COLOR FOR INTERIORS
Historical and Modern

An essential reference work covering the major period styles of history and including modern palettes for the authentic decoration of homes, institutional and commercial interiors **by Faber Birren**

Whitney Library of Design, New York

Library of Congress Catalog Card No. 63-11888
© Whitney Library of Design,
Charles E. Whitney, President;
William Wilson Atkin, Vice-President
A Division of Whitney Publications, Inc.
18 East 50th Street, New York, N. Y. 10022
Publishers of Interiors and Industrial Design

TABLE OF CONTENTS

TO ERIC AND STELLA

FOREWORD

This is meant to be a practical book written around a very human subject—color. For a good part of my life as a professional colorist, I have taken any number of busman's holidays into the dim and historic past. I have been constantly fascinated and struck by the fact that color has touched upon virtually every aspect of human life and culture since the beginning of time.

Origins have been of great interest to me—plus, of course, the whole curious effect of color in human life. Because all colors exist at all times, so to speak, it becomes something of a scholarly and technical job to get down to cases, to analyze, screen, and otherwise sort out the changing courses and directions of man's preferences during different ages and periods. Nothing here is ever static. Thus if there were anything authentic or individual to certain generations or centuries I wanted to record them. Except for ancient times when symbolism dominated creative impulse—and the palette was simple —I encountered a jumble of facts about color which only patience and careful deduction could unravel. The results of this research are in the first and historic section of this book.

The second section, devoted to modern principles of color, speaks for itself. It represents an outgrowth of clinical, physiological, and psychological inquiry into the subject. As modern man has learned, if the appeal of color is natural, spontaneous, and intuitive, there must be more to it than merely greets the eye. This conclusion has been sound, and acknowledgment of it has led (and will lead further) to a truly dynamic and practical application of color in modern life.

Out of this effort has come a rather curious observation. Western man has tended to be self-conscious about color. Possibly because of a Puritanical background, color to him has been a matter of sensuous indulgence. Many a person, even today, feels a certain audacity in bright hues. Architects who apply color to the exterior of buildings (even pseudo-Greek temples which were originally in full color) find themselves on the defensive. If they do not feel a guilty conscience, at least they are quite aware that they face much prejudice. In interior design and decoration, where color is common enough, restraint is far more prevalent than simple abandonment to impulse.

Man is getting over his inhibitions as to color. He should know that color vision itself is a wholly natural endowment, presented to man, not for its esthetic delights, but to condition him to his environment and aid his survival. He should further know that for thousands of years prior to the Reformation (when timidity and prudery were imposed upon him), color was an intimate part of life and not a mere embellishment to it. It was a necessity and not a luxury. It covered his buildings inside and out, his statues, garments, furnishings. It was related to his religions, and governments, to healing and medicine, to his rituals and rites—to just about everything, in fact. It belonged to every man and not to the artist alone. It was as natural to his culture as to nature herself. He was not in the least sophisticated about it. It was pure need to him and not affectation.

In the brief notes of this book—and in the all-important color charts—the records of the past have been set forth. They are as authentic as I could make them. They picture man's life, *in color*, as he felt inspired and moved at various times. While they are handy as reference sources, it is my hope that the historical circumstances that surrounded them (and which they indeed surrounded) will also hold a measure of attraction to the reader.

Faber Birren

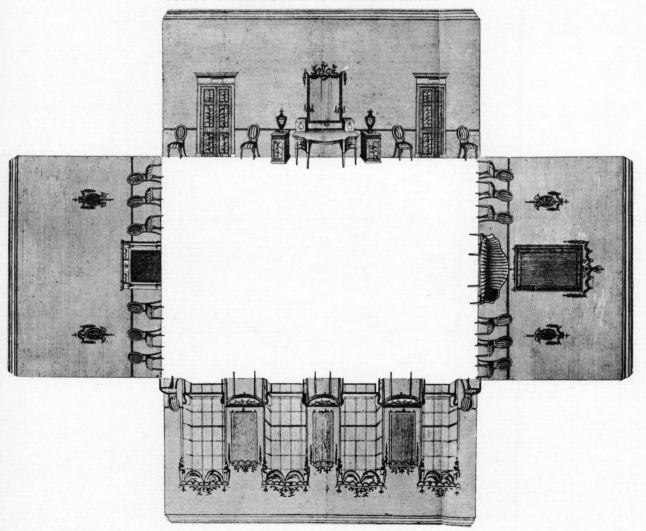

1 THE CLASSICAL TRADITION AND THE CREATIVE TRADITION

A literal duplication of the colors of antiquity may not always reveal either what ancient man did centuries ago or what he had in mind. Obviously color will fade after hundreds and thousands of years. A good job of scholarship requires not alone a study of surviving relics but of historical and literary sources which explain ancient viewpoints.

In America, for example, one may often be amused to read descriptions of the paintings, ceramics, and textiles of the Indian. The observer, lost to what he sees, may reach the wholly erroneous conclusion that the Indian has precious and subtle taste in color. The truth, however, is that he used pigments and dyes made of minerals, bones, roots, bark, fruit and was naturally limited in his expression. When aniline dyes were introduced not too many years ago, there was a sudden burst of brilliant magenta, sulphur yellow, peacock blue in his handiwork. This is what he really liked and had been trying to do all the time!

What has been lost in the shuffle of history is the fact that ancient man was not a creative artist as we understand things today. He had little if any interest in expressing his personal

taste. Virtually everything he did related to symbolism, to uses for color that were set and prescribed by the Mysteries. He was by no means toying with visual and emotional delights but with deep meanings, with practical uses for color that would protect his body on earth and preserve his soul in the hereafter.

To understand traditions in color it is necessary to appreciate that for a good many centuries (more or less up to the Renaissance) man had concrete notions about color and decoration and seldom gave himself to the abstract. The cave drawings of Upper Paleolithic man — which antedate recorded history by several thousand years—were concerned with animals and hunters. Here color means little, for the palette was limited to crude mineral pigments. When recorded history begins (around 4000 B. C.) symbolic uses for color immediately appear and continue to survive for many centuries.

This book distinguishes between a Classical tradition for color and a Creative tradition; these, as will be seen, mark the entire course of color in decoration and period styles. In another book by the author, *Color, a Pictorial*

Survey in Words and Pictures (University Books, 1963), a wealth of evidence is presented on color meanings. To the ancient, color was identified with the universe and heavens; with his gods; the elements of science; the points of the compass; the sun, moon, stars, and planets. It was an essential part of his religion, of healing. His temples and art forms were devoted to history and mythology, and each color applied had a symbolic meaning and purpose. Color marked the ceremonies of birth, marriage, and death. Jewelry consisted of amulets fashioned in symbolic colors. Clothing was worn in different hues to denote caste or rank. There are survivals of this in heraldry and in rituals of Jewish and Roman Catholic rites. Otherwise. much has been lost.

In architecture and decoration, color symbolism prevailed. Egyptian temples were veritable charts of the mysteries. One of the oldest known buildings, the Mountain of God at Ur (2300 B. C.), consisted of a tower built in four stages, each decorated with a different hue. According to C. Leonard Woolley, ''These colors had mystical significance and stood for the various divisions of the universe, the dark

HERE IN THE VILLA MEDICI IN ROME IS THE CREATIVE TRADITION OF THE RENAISSANCE IN WHICH, ALTHOUGH CLASSICAL IDEALS WERE REBORN, ARCHITECTURAL AND DECORATIVE STYLES WERE UNIQUE AND ORIGINAL TO THE AGE. PHOTOGRAPH COURTESY WARE MEMORIAL LIBRARY, COLUMBIA UNIVERSITY.

THE PALAZZO REZZONICO IN VENICE IS AN EXAMPLE OF HOW THE CREATIVE ARTIST OF THE RENAISSANCE TOOK GREEK AND ROMAN ELEMENTS AND GAVE THEM ELABORATE DEVELOPMENT. EXTERIOR ARCHITECTURE FEATURED SCULPTURE; INTERIOR DESIGN FEATURED PAINTING. PHOTOGRAPH COURTESY WARE MEMORIAL LIBRARY, COLUMBIA UNIVERSITY.

VERSAILLES, THE CLASSICAL AND THE CREATIVE, SIDE BY SIDE, WITH LOUIS XIV BETWEEN. THE OLDER BUILDINGS ARE TO THE RIGHT, THE NEWER ONES TO THE LEFT. THIS RADICAL CHANGE OF TASTE TOOK PLACE WITHIN A FEW YEARS. PHOTOGRAPH BY TOM DOUGLAS JONES.

THE CAPITOL AT COLONIAL WILLIAMSBURG, RESTORED TO ITS EARLY EIGHTEENTH CENTURY APPEARANCE. THIS IS ENGLISH GEORGIAN ARCHITECTURE AT ITS BEST AND SHORTLY BEFORE THE CLASSICAL TRADITION WAS REVIVED—THERE ARE NO GREEK COLUMNS. COLONIAL WILLIAMSBURG PHOTOGRAPH.

IN CONTRAST TO THE CAPITOL AT WILLIAMSBURG, HERE IS THE U. S. CAPITOL AT WASHINGTON, D. C. IT WAS IN 1762—AND AFTER —THAT EXCAVATIONS AT POMPEII REVIVED CLASSICAL IDEAS AND LED TO PSEUDO-GREEK AND PSEUDO-ROMAN STYLES. PHOTOGRAPH COURTESY WASHINGTON CONVENTION AND VISITORS BUREAU.

underworld, the habitable earth, the heavens, and the sun." A similar *ziggurat*, or Tower of Babel, was described by Herodotus, and each of seven stages had a different color. In modern times James Fergusson wrote, "This temple, as we know from the decipherment of the cylinders which are found on its angles, was dedicated to the seven planets or heavenly spheres, and we find it consequently adorned with the colors of each."

Here is the point: for probably 4,000 years man respected the Classical tradition and used the spectrum as a sort of color guide to his beliefs. For only 600 years or so has he indulged himself in the Creative tradition—and yet most persons have assumed this tradition to exist from all time!

To clarify the matter and proceed with the purposes of this book, consider the following.

The Classical tradition means simplicity and directness with color. It derives from ancient times when the color palette was restricted, and all hues had definite significance. Although it staggered at times and apparently expired during the Renaissance, it was later revived—but with its original meanings lost. (As will be mentioned later, such a revival occurred in the eighteenth century and right in the midst of the great period styles of England, France, and America.)

The Creative tradition, on the other hand, had its origin during the Renaissance and after. It has no concern with symbolism. Its spirit was that of the great age of enlightenment. Through the release of philosophy, science, humanism, reformation in religion, world ex-

ploration, the invention of oil painting, and amazing developments in all the decorative arts, man sought freedom and individuality and threw off the burdens of his past. It is then that the art of color abandoned simplicity. Men were to delve into the mysterious depths of their psyches and search for that which was new, different, unique, highly personal. Color expression was in consequence to become elegant, complex, and elaborate.

Where color is to symbolize, it must of necessity be clear and simple—red, yellow, green, blue, purple. Where it is born of individual interpretation it naturally becomes more sophisticated and subtle. Renaissance brocades are lush with purples and violets, yellow-greens, blue-greens, olive-greens, golds, and tans; colors which obviously were intended to break with conventions and not conform to them.

It was the Creative tradition of the Renaissance that moved across Europe and influenced the magnificent period styles of Western nations, particularly France. From this spirit came baroque styles, elaborate tapesteries, textiles, rugs, wall decorations, wallpaper, importations from China and the Orient, all to indulge man in an abandoned and sensuous spree of color.

Then Puritanical influences and the excavations of one Johann Winckelmann in Italy in the latter part of the eighteenth century brought man face to face again with the Classical. After which the two traditions collided, melded, and then traveled together in a friendly way up to the present.

2 THE BEGINNINGS, EGYPT, GREECE, ROME

For reasons already explained, the Classical palette of antiquity was a simple one. Western culture traces from Egypt into Asia Minor and thence to Greece, Rome, and on up through Europe—with occasional excursions, of course, into India, China, and the Orient. Because emphasis in color and decoration was on symbolism, it is clear—and written record bears this out—that the artist had simple and precise notions about the spectrum. And this attitude prevailed for many centuries.

The Egyptian was a member of the red race and prided himself on the distinction. The use of cosmetics probably had its origin here, for dyes and pigments were applied to the skin, not alone to beautify but proclaim pride in the hue. There are still vestiges of red paint on the face of the Sphinx.

Egyptian gods were identified with different hues. Osiris was symbolized by green, his wife Isis by blue, their son Horus by white. Pharoah wore a white crown for his dominion over upper Egypt and a red crown for lower Egypt. There are fascinating and elaborate tokens of color in amulets and charms that could be quoted endlessly. In speaking of

AN EGYPTIAN PAINT BOX OF THE FIFTEENTH CENTURY B.C. FROM WHICH CAN BE SEEN THE LIMITED NUMBER OF HUES EMPLOYED BY THE ANCIENT DECORATOR. COLORS WERE APPLIED IN FLAT AREAS AND SELDOM MIXED. PHOTOGRAPH COURTESY THE METROPOLITAN MUSEUM OF ART, ROGERS FUND, 1948.

AN EGYPTIAN INTERIOR AS IT WAS VISUALIZED IN A FRENCH LITHOGRAPH OF THE LATE NINETEENTH CENTURY. THE COLORS WERE PRIMARY IN NATURE AND RESPECTED SYMBOLIC TRADITIONS. PHOTOGRAPH COURTESY NEW YORK PUBLIC LIBRARY PICTURE COLLECTION.

Egyptian vignettes in the *Book of the Dead*, E. A. Wallis Budge remarks that they likely "had nothing to do with artistic ideas or development. That object was to benefit the dead by magical means."

Man today may feel apart from ancient lore and may confuse what to him seems romantic with that which to the ancient was quite the contrary. Today in the bazaars of Cairo one may still see colorful beads and ornaments worn by men and beasts. They may seem decorative and quaint; as Budge remarks, they were originally intended to avert the evil eye "but this fact has been forgotten, and amulets have degenerated into mere ornaments."

The Egyptian decorative palette is shown on Chart 1. These colors were applied to great temples, such as Karnak and Luxor. Red was associated with the Egyptian race. The ceilings of temples were blue and usually embellished with drawings of the constellations. The floors were green like the meadows of the Nile. Purple, however, was often used as being emblematic of earth.

The colors, then, are direct and simple, and the record is unusually accurate; examples of Egyptian coloring exist in great abundance and will be found in museums everywhere. Shown on page 6 in black and white is an Egyptian paint box or palette from the Metropolitan Museum in New York dating back to the fifteenth century B.C. and in which the colors are still preserved. This particular box, with its eight compartments, contains a terra cotta red, light and medium yellow ocher, turquoise blue, green, white, black, and one empty compartment which probably held a blue or purple. Similar paint boxes—but without the preserved colors—are to be seen at the British Museum in London; they are made of wood or stone and contain from eight to fourteen wells.

It is known that the Egyptian used tempera paints composed of mineral pigments mixed with a gum or other binding vehicle. There was carbon for black, cobalt for blue, malachite for green, red and yellow ocher, oxide of iron for pink and red, arsenic trisulfide which made a brilliant lemon yellow, crystalline compounds of silica, copper, and calcium. The art of color making reached a high stage of development indeed in Ancient Egypt, for the surviving record is still clear.

In the color terms used on Chart 1 (page 23), Rust Red, Henna Red, and Dull Gold were used for flesh tones, the red tint for men and the yellow tint for women. Large areas were often Bone Ivory. There was strong decorative use of Medium and Deep Colbalt, Deep Luxor Green, Sun Yellow, Soft Purple. (The purple standard on Chart 1 probably derives from a purer original hue.) Garments were frequently painted in Pale Cobalt, Pale Luxor Green, Horizon Blue, Alabaster Pink. Black for outlines and for hair was the rule.

These colors carried over into Asia Minor and proceeded to Greece and Rome with little change, for their symbolism also carried over. They are found, for example, in the temple at Khorsabad of ancient Babylon, and in the Parthenon at Athens. When the archaeologists in later days made excavations, when anti-

quarians and adventurers long after the Renaissance (Napoleon was one of them) dug into venerable hills, mountains, and deserts, this Classical "taste" was refreshed and revived—but with old sentiments and superstitions either overlooked or disregarded.

Because of its wetter climate, the color record from Greece is less authentic. Scholars and archaeologists, recording freshly unearthed ruins, made accurate notations in the latter part of the nineteenth century. Carefully supervised lithographic reproductions were then made. While some of them may be exaggerated, there is no question as to the common and widespread use of color in Greek architecture and decoration.

No ancient culture has had a stronger influence on Western civilization than that of Greece. Modern architects and interior designers may be reluctant or embarrassed to admit it, but Greek ideals of design and decoration still prevail. It seems next to impossible to create beauty of form and line without running into the genius of the ancient Greek. Yet while there is full awareness of the majesty of Greek design, knowledge of Greek color is negligible. This is because the forms have been repeated over and over, but with the original colors stripped away. As a matter of fact, a clear knowledge of Greek color did not impress itself upon the world until a few generations ago. And when the true facts were known, many were incensed. Rodin is said to have struck his breast and shouted, "I feel in here that these were never colored!" Frank Lloyd Wright, with equal disdain, abused the Greek as being the original "inferior desecrator." This attitude traces directly from the Reformation when color was suddenly removed and withdrawn from much of architecture as a sensuous and pagan vice.

A naive mind, visiting Washington, D.C., where there is a vast assemblage of classical architecture, might well assume that the temples of Greece were of natural stone and marble. The enlightened mind might know otherwise and yet still resent the original fact of color. How could the Greek with such a sensitive eye for form, smear bright coatings over his graceful columns, capitals, relief ornaments, and sculpture? The answer, quite simply, is that color was a symbolic element in his creations, not a fanciful one. It would have been wholly unnatural for him *not* to use color.

Lest the writer be accused of undue prejudice—or slanted interpretations—in favor of color, here are a few excerpts from scholars. What they say may come as a surprise to many.

C. W. Ceram: "The plastic works of the ancient Greeks were gaily colored. Statuary was deeply dyed with garish pigments. The marble figure of a woman found on the Athenian Acropolis was tinctured red, green, blue, and yellow. Quite often statues had red lips, glowing eyes made of precious stones, and even artificial eyelashes."

Describing a freshly unearthed Greek pediment (author unknown): "Flesh, reddish in tone; globe of eyes yellow, iris green, with a hole in the center filled with black; black outlines to eyebrows and eyelids; hair and beard bright blue at the time of excavation, which disintegrated later to a greenish tone; circle of brown around the nipples."

Frederik Poulsen: "When the reliefs were discovered, they were richly painted, and still the colors have not all faded. As was indicated in the treatment of the metopes of the Sicyonian Treasury, the background was blue. The figures are treated in blue, green, and red, the last color in two shades, light red and golden-red. The clothes are red with blue borders, while the colors are changed when two or more articles of clothing or armor are worn. The helmets are blue, with red ornamental stripes on the edges, to pick them out from the blue background; the last features remind one of the little red nimbus which in red-figured vases divides the dark hair of the figures from the dark ground. The outsides of the shields are alternately blue and red, their insides red, with a narrow colorless border along the edge, a color scheme answering exactly to that of figures on the Aeginetan pediment. The bodies of Cybele's lions are colorless, but the manes, harness, and yoke are red. The tails and manes of the horses are red, or where several are seen close together, alternately red and blue."

Sir William Beechey: "We observe that the practice we allude to [the use of the same colors on the same elements] does not appear . . . to be the result of any occasional caprice or fancy, but of a generally established system; for the colors of the several parts do not seem to have materially varied in any two instances with which we are acquainted. . . . We can scarcely doubt that one particular color was appropriated by general consent or practice to each of the several parts of the buildings."

Here then, is the Classical tradition at its strictest if not best. If the Greek was the true creative artist with form and design, he quite apparently, unlike the artist of the Renaissance, took instruction as to color and saw little need to revolt.

Chart 2 (page 25) shows the Greek palette. There is great resemblance to that of Egypt. Large exterior and interior surfaces were often coated with Ivory White. As already described in a few quotations, bright red, blue, and green were used in decoration. In the famous Parthenon frieze the background to the relief figures was Scarlet. Stellar Blue was given prominence

THIS IS A WALL PAINTING FROM POMPEII, FIRST CENTURY B.C. THE CENTRAL WALL PANELS WERE BRIGHT RED. OTHER DECORATIVE ELEMENTS WERE GOLDEN YELLOW, DEEP BROWN, LIGHT CLEAR GREEN. PHOTOGRAPH COURTESY THE METROPOLITAN MUSEUM OF ART, ROGERS FUND, 1903.

in wide panels. The figures themselves were realistically tinted with Mist Blue, Pale Malachite, Marble Pink, and Sun Yellow.

Greek culture was carried to Rome through philosophy, political theories, gods, science, and colors. Symbolism began to fade, but only partially. As a matter of fact, there is written evidence that a good number of early painters and decorators came from Greece and were put to work because of their knowledge and skill with color. The Romans were builders at heart and made more lavish use of raw materials, marbles in bright hues, gold, bronze, mosaics. The gods, however, were still identified by color. Purple, the imperial color of Rome, was in reality a Magenta and was sometimes referred to as Red. It traces from Greece and is described by Richard Payne Knight: "The bodies of Roman Consuls and Dictators were painted red during the sacred ceremony of the triumph, and from this custom the imperial purple of later ages is derived." The emperor in his purple (or red) robes, embroidered or spangled with gold, was the personification of Jupiter. His chariot was drawn by white horses. A wreath of laurel was upon his head.

IN THIS VIEW OF WALL PAINTINGS FROM BOSCOREALE AT POMPEII THE WALL PANELS WERE ROSE, WITH GREEN WREATHS IN FAIRLY NATURALISTIC STYLE. OTHER COLORS WERE IVORY, GOLD, DEEP BROWN. PHOTOGRAPH COURTESY THE METROPOLITAN MUSEUM OF ART, ROGERS FUND, 1903.

His face was reddened with vermilion.

Roman ruins disintegrated, as did the Greek. However, there were the remarkable exceptions of Pompeii and Herculaneum.

It was in August of 79 A.D. that Vesuvius erupted without warning. The top of the mountain split apart, and a flood of volcanic ash, smoke, and lethal gas buried the cities and their inhabitants, apparently in an instant.

What seems incredible today is that seventeen hundred years elapsed before Pompeii and Herculaneum were substantially unearthed. Except for the inroads of a few venturesome and haphazard diggers, the civilization lay buried all during the Renaissance itself. Little of what it held was seen by the masters of Italy or Europe. Both Gothic and Renaissance art and architecture flourished and took directions of their own while the two Roman cities lay undiscovered and preserved, as in a locked museum.

It was Johann Winckelmann who first devoted himself to the task of excavation during the middle of the eighteenth century. (A bit of digging had been done previously in 1737.) Soon light of day fell upon architectural splen-

dors, rows of houses, temples, theaters, tablets, papyrus rolls, jewelry, utensils, wall paintings, frescoes, all fresh with color.

The color record of Pompeii and Herculaneum is exceptionally complete and the palette, shown on Chart 3 (page 27), is in the Classical tradition. There is a bold and uninhibited use of bright colors and deep colors, including black, in large area and over entire walls—offset by painted decoration and ornament. While some of the tones are fresher than in Egypt and Greece (Rich Gold, Rich Coral, the Pompeii Greens), it is surely no coincidence that the Classical tradition still prevailed.

Rome, of course, endured for many centuries. In latter years before the Dark Ages (eighth century), decoration became less formal and more naturalistic. Even more significant, the influence of Christianity increased, and Roman gods and mythology were replaced by Christian saints. While color symbolism was attached to early Christian art (and is still preserved in Roman Catholic ritual), fresco paintings on walls and ceilings, frequently with off-white grounds, became realistic in nature and began to foreshadow the Renaissance. Symbolism faded, and the more creative artist, expressing his own individuality, was to inspire a revolution in architectural decoration.

The Classical tradition, however, was not lost forever. As will be mentioned again later, Winckelmann's findings at Pompeii and Herculaneum and his monumental works which began to appear in 1762, caused an eruption of their own in interior decoration. What the Renaissance had brought to Versailles, for example, was suddenly dropped, and interior artists of the day scurried back into the distant past. The Classical tradition, which had once ruled decoration but which had been by-passed by the Creative tradition of the Renaissance, came back into eminence. That which was as old as antiquity became suddenly new. For that matter, most of the world had never seen it.

3 THE FREEDOM OF THE RENAISSANCE

Much of the color and decoration of antiquity has crumbled and will be found recorded only in museum restorations and the scholarly works of archaeologists. The traveler who visits the temples of Egypt or Greece, or the forum at Rome, will be impressed chiefly by the majesty of their architecture in form and design, for the colors that once adorned them have faded and deteriorated.

The Renaissance, however, blatantly exists in all its lavish splendor. Baroque ornament, marble, gold leaf, murals, mosaics, frescoes, paintings, sculpture, carved furniture, tapestries, textiles overpower the senses and leave the eye and emotions exhausted.

The word Renaissance (renascence) means, of course, rebirth. The movement began in Italy and soon spread throughout the western world. This sudden reverence for Greek and Roman art and culture met the medieval Gothic style head on, stopped or at least slowed it down, and then moved like a brush fire across Europe, Spain, and England. A true Gothic feeling had not, after all, made much progress in Italy.

The Middle Ages were over. With changes

in political and economic conditions, a substantial middle class of merchants and bankers developed and had plenty of money to spend. Religious fervor, supported by a militant and wealthy church, also lent patronage. Social life began to approach a structure recognizable in modern times.

Renaissance buildings and palaces were for the most part designed to feature works of art and are lost without them. Alcoves and niches are made for sculpture, bordered moldings on walls and ceilings for paintings. Everywhere there is a profusion of detail, with empty space virtually unknown. Although the whole mythology and spirit of Christianity dominates the period, its outward religious expression is frankly pagan.

There is little doubt but that the art of oil painting had much to do with a sudden fascination with color. Anything could be done —and was done. Yet when Renaissance interior decoration is screened or digested it contains, for all its luxury, definite echoes from Greece and Rome. As one example, in a carefully researched and restored version of an elaborate ceiling in the Apartamento Borgia of the Vatican one sees the scarlet red, bright emerald green, cobalt blue, and gold of ancient times. This might be coincidence, but it is hardly likely. According to the writings of the Italian architect and historian, Vasari (and others), the ceiling included much allegorical symbolism from Greece and Rome—centaurs, mythological birds and animals, signs of the zodiac, and the like—leading to the very logical conclusion that if ancient motifs were re-

CARRACCIO'S HALL IN THE PALAZZO FARNESE, ROME, IS THE TYPICAL RENAISSANCE INTERIOR. ARCHITECTURE AND INTERIOR DESIGN ARE DEVOTED TO THE DISPLAY OF WORKS OF ART. NOTHING IS PLAIN. PHOTOGRAPH COURTESY ITALIAN STATE TOURIST OFFICE.

IN THIS PICTURE GALLERY IN THE PALAZZO COLONNA, ROME, DECORATION, AGAIN, IS A FRAME FOR THE ARTS. THERE IS EXTRAVAGANT USE OF MARBLE AND GILT. PHOTOGRAPH COURTESY ITALIAN STATE TOURIST OFFICE.

peated, so were their hues.

Yet if the Classical tradition was still extant during the Renaissance the artists of the time soon forgot about it and lost themselves to the greatest orgy of color known to history. For out of the Renaissance, out of man's search for personal values, came the Creative tradition which in principle and spirit still guides cultural expression today. (If one thinks of oriental color as sensuous, let him be advised that it is symbolic before it is anything else. Even today, the color expression of China and Japan still adheres to strict custom and ritual. Artists seldom take license with it.)

To differentiate between the Classical and the Creative traditions: the colors that a person might choose for a flag, a crest of some sort, or the class colors of graduation, will be studied for their venerable meanings; the researcher may consult heraldry or the recognized tokens of religious rite or education. Yet the same person choosing colors for the living room of a home will either follow the vogues of fashion or indulge in personal fancies.

Thus in the Classical tradition, the colors are usually simpler and fewer in number. There is a tendency to reduce the complex world of color to precise elements. In the Creative tradition the sky is the limit. There is a tendency to get away from the primary and to seek that which is different, original, exclusive, subtle, sophisticated.

Chart 4 (page 29) shows Renaissance colors. They will be found to resemble the colors of Egypt, Greece, and Rome. Bear in mind, however, that the standards shown were basi-cally used for decorative purposes. Above and beyond them was the full palette of the Italian painter in which he mixed just about every color to adorn interiors with religious, mythological, and fanciful subjects.

To get the spirit of Renaissance decoration, appreciate that virtually nothing was plain. One must wait a couple of centuries, beyond the Baroque and Rococo styles, for a revival of the Classical tradition and a return to formality and simplicity. Yet in the Renaissance, creative originality in color had its truly first great epoch—the result not only of competent developments in the manufacture of dyestuffs and pigments, but of the personal desires of artists to express inner compulsions, dreams, and insights. Now color would become a highly personal art, and decoration would cater to the boundless domain of taste and emotion as sensed within the human psyche and not as directed by any outside convention or authority, religious or otherwise.

There are many features peculiar to Renaissance decoration. One is a lavish use of gold, not only for ornament but for large areas on which decorations were applied. There is much use of paintings, moldings, pilasters, columns, capitals, cornices, carving, marquetry in imitation of mosaic and inlaid marble. Wall areas may be rich and dark or off-white but they are rarely subtle, pastel, or muted. All is extroverted and sensuous—including the spiritual. If the Greeks had a golden age in the philosophical sense, the Italian Renaissance had one in the material.

In textiles, the period of the Renaissance

revolutionized the art for centuries to follow. Here are a few color schemes taken from Italian brocades.

Purple and yellowish green ornaments on blue-violet ground; outlines in gold.

Dull crimson, pale blue, and yellow ornaments on dark gray ground.

Pale yellow-green ornaments on deep amber ground.

Light yellow-green and dark blue-green ornaments on deep crimson ground.

Pale blue-green ornaments on dark gray-blue ground, with touches of white and gold.

Emerald green and dull orange ornaments on dark gray-green ground; outlines in gold.

Refer now to Chart 4 (page 29) which shows typical and well documented colors for wall decoration of the Italian Renaissance. They definitely echo Egypt, Greece, and ancient Rome when seen out of context. However, these settings bear very little resemblance to the past. That is, if Greek ideals were cherished, they were also embellished and made fantastically intricate and sophisticated.

Ivory White and Marble Cream were often used for whatever blank spaces might exist or as backgrounds to colorful ornaments. Metallic Gold was everywhere. There was no hesitancy in the use of Pompeii Red, Medium Malachite, Golden Ocher, Della Robbia Blue. The artist discovered that deep hues like Deep Malachite, Deep Cobalt, Garnet Red, and brown and copper tones made dramatic foils for a full spectrum of pure and tinted colors. Spaces were large, life vigorous and outgoing.

It would take the French and the English to

HERE IS A FRENCH HALL OF THE EARLY SIXTEENTH CENTURY WITH A MIXTURE OF MEDIEVAL, GOTHIC, AND RENAISSANCE STYLES. COLOR IS USED MAINLY IN TEXTILES AND TAPESTRIES. PHOTOGRAPH COURTESY THORNE EUROPEAN ROOMS IN MINIATURE, THE ART INSTITUTE OF CHICAGO.

IN THIS ORNATE VENETIAN BEDROOM OF THE RENAISSANCE PE-
RIOD, THE WALLS ARE SILK BROCADE IN A RICH GOLD COLOR.
MUCH OF THE ROCOCO ORNAMENT IS GILDED. PHOTOGRAPH
COURTESY THE METROPOLITAN MUSEUM OF ART.

THIS FRENCH BEDROOM OF THE LATE SIXTEENTH CENTURY IS IN
THE STYLE FIRST INTRODUCED INTO FRANCE FROM ITALY BY
FRANCIS I. PHOTOGRAPH COURTESY THORNE EUROPEAN ROOMS
IN MINIATURE, THE ART INSTITUTE OF CHICAGO.

refine the Renaissance, think in terms of smaller rooms that required less vividness, and thus introduce those more intimate pastels and muted hues which the world has now come to associate with modern interior decoration.

Renaissance expression was vigorous and appropriate to its time. Seen today either in its original glory or in museum restoration, however, it appears unduly ornate and effusive. Much of this pretentiousness has to be stripped away to adapt the best features of the age to modern taste.

THIS IS THE DINING ROOM OF I. TATTI, A VILLA AT SETTIGNANO IN ITALY OWNED BY THE LATE EMINENT ART AUTHORITY, BERNARD BERENSON. SOMEWHAT PROVINCIAL IN ITS SIMPLICITY, ALL DETAILS HAVE BEEN PRESERVED TO DISTINGUISH A SEVENTEENTH CENTURY INTERIOR. PHOTOGRAPH COURTESY ANTIQUES MAGAZINE.

A ROOM IN THE FAMOUS KRONBORG CASTLE OF ELSINORE, IMMORTALIZED BY SHAKESPEARE IN HAMLET. THIS IS THE RENAISSANCE BROUGHT TO DENMARK IN THE SEVENTEENTH CENTURY BUT STRIPPED OF OSTENTATION. PHOTOGRAPH BY MARTIN LOWENFISH.

Note on the Color Charts

For purposes of accuracy and convenience in color matching, the various traditional and modern standards described in this book are presented in the form of actual paint chips. While they refer chiefly to colors used on walls and woodwork, they also reflect taste in wallpaper and wallcoverings, textiles, painted floors, and carpeting, as distinct for each period or use set forth.

How authentic are they? It would be wholly erroneous and academic to assume that the craftsmen of the past followed scientific methods and used precisely certain hues at certain times. While many colors shown on the charts have been matched against originals and restorations, for the most part an effort has been made to identify the *spirit* of the time. Were the colors light, dark, pure, grayish, and what were their hues?

On the matter of authenticity, one frequently sees textiles, tapestries, brocades, needlepoint in which the craftsman has meticulously matched faded yarns. Is one to respect the once living past or the dead ghost of it? The same is true of paints and wallpapers. One may be sure that the decorator of old was human. If he preferred certain tones of putty gray, soft yellowish green, dull terra cotta, he was forced to mix his colors every time he applied them, and what he applied differed at least slightly on each occasion that he wielded his brush. Besides, many of the pigments he used were fugitive and they materially faded over the years.

The same holds true today. It can be said on good evidence that ivory was a popular American color around 1940, green around 1950, and beige around 1960. But who could state categorically that only a certain tone of ivory, green, or beige distinguished the time?

If there are no authentic colors in the strictest and most limited meaning of the word, there definitely are authentic *kinds and types* of colors. What is important to this book is the over-all character of a given period — or a statement of principles in the case of modern color usage. Wherever possible, of course, and wherever fair and reasonable, the colors of the past have been literally matched from well preserved specimens. In all instances, however, the attitude has been faithful and genuine and not pedantic.

CHART 1 FOR CHAPTER 2

These are the major colors of the Egyptian tradition, taken mainly from actual decorations found on tombs, sculpture, coffins, wall paintings, etc. Being Classical in nature, and adhering to Egyptian symbolism and mysticism, they were used, virtually without change, over a period of nearly three thousand years of ancient Egyptian history from 3000 to 500 B.C. They are still well preserved after two thousand more years of survival.

Although the color samples have been accurately reproduced in permanent pigments, they should be handled with care and not unduly exposed to light.

ANCIENT EGYPT

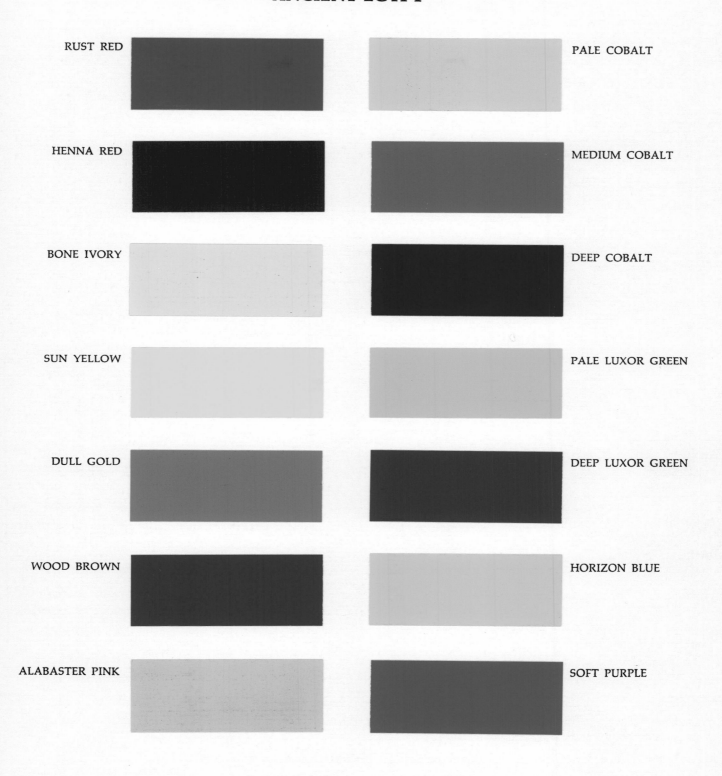

RUST RED

HENNA RED

BONE IVORY

SUN YELLOW

DULL GOLD

WOOD BROWN

ALABASTER PINK

PALE COBALT

MEDIUM COBALT

DEEP COBALT

PALE LUXOR GREEN

DEEP LUXOR GREEN

HORIZON BLUE

SOFT PURPLE

CHART 2 FOR CHAPTER 2

Like the Egyptians, the Greeks followed the Classical tradition and adhered to a set palette of colors which showed little change over three or four centuries. In architecture and decoration, emphasis was on symbolism, the same colors being used in the same places according to prescribed practice. The colors herewith are taken mostly from archaeological records of fresh unearthings—which have since faded.

ANCIENT GREECE

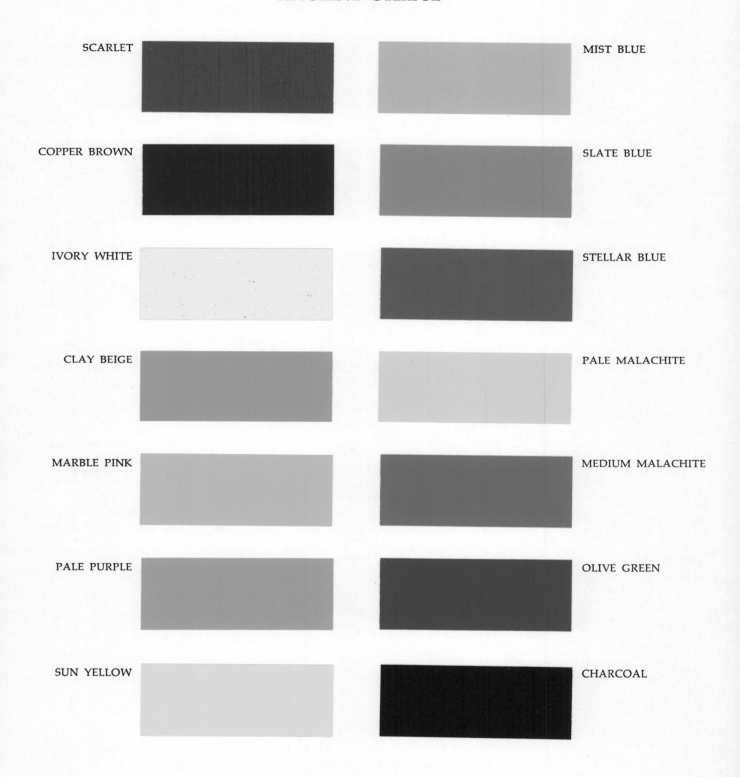

SCARLET	MIST BLUE
COPPER BROWN	SLATE BLUE
IVORY WHITE	STELLAR BLUE
CLAY BEIGE	PALE MALACHITE
MARBLE PINK	MEDIUM MALACHITE
PALE PURPLE	OLIVE GREEN
SUN YELLOW	CHARCOAL

CHART 3 FOR CHAPTER 2

Because of the more humid climate of Italy, surviving colors have materially faded. The samples shown here are mainly from archaeological records made at the time of excavations at Pompeii and Herculaneum. These civilizations date to the first century A.D. The reproductions are both accurate and historical. The tradition is still Classical and formal and involves a limited palette.

EARLY ROMAN

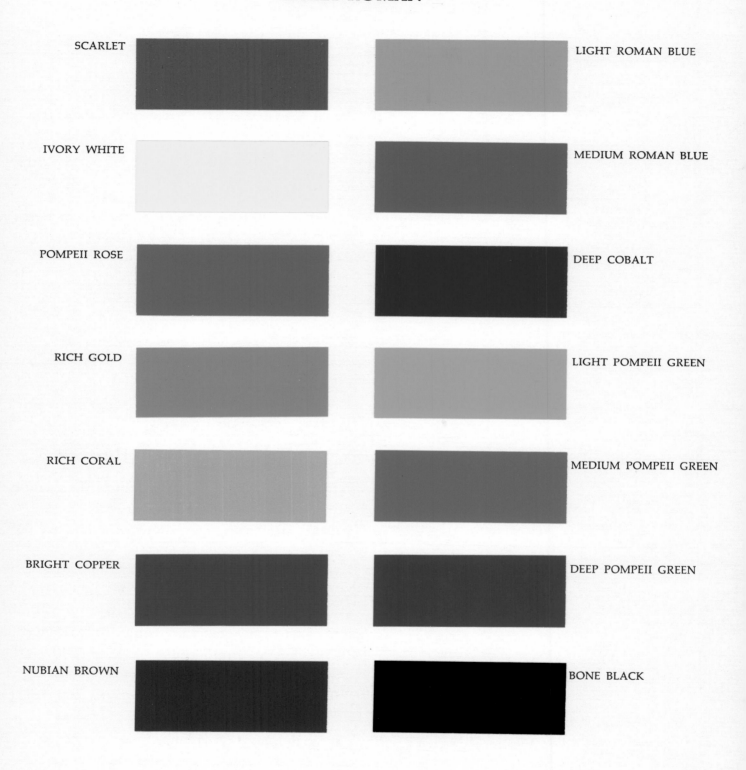

SCARLET

IVORY WHITE

POMPEII ROSE

RICH GOLD

RICH CORAL

BRIGHT COPPER

NUBIAN BROWN

LIGHT ROMAN BLUE

MEDIUM ROMAN BLUE

DEEP COBALT

LIGHT POMPEII GREEN

MEDIUM POMPEII GREEN

DEEP POMPEII GREEN

BONE BLACK

CHART 4 FOR CHAPTER 3

Renaissance colors still exist in their original form and reproduction of them is therefore accurate. The samples shown on this chart, however, refer to colors as used in architecture and decoration—not in the art of oil painting. Because the Classical traditions of Greece and ancient Rome were respected during the fifteenth and sixteenth century Renaissance, the colors are quite similar to those of the earlier civilizations.

THE RENAISSANCE

METALLIC GOLD

MEDIUM MALACHITE

GOLDEN OCHER

DEEP MALACHITE

MARBLE CREAM

CERAMIC BLUE

IVORY WHITE

DELLA ROBBIA BLUE

POMPEII RED

DEEP COBALT

BRIGHT COPPER

GARNET RED

DULL BROWN

RICH BROWN

CHART 5 FOR CHAPTER 4

This chart show a few Renaissance influences. Mostly, however, it features colors created during the reigns of Louis XIV and XV—up to 1774. Notable are the pastels introduced and glorified by Madame de Pompadour. This brought the Classical tradition of formality and adherence to ritual to an end. The Creative tradition, initiated during the Renaissance, met full flower in France.

FRENCH UP THROUGH LOUIS XV

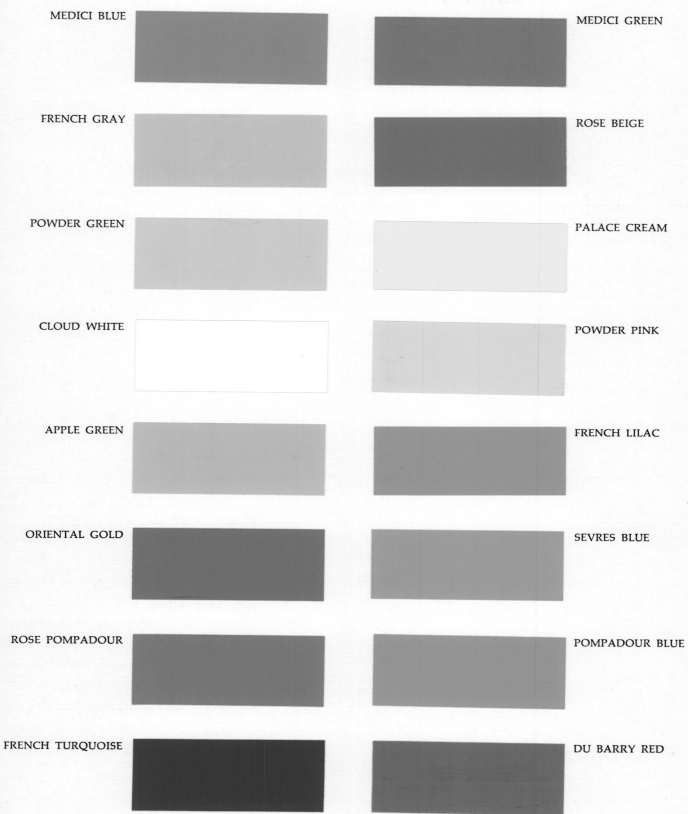

MEDICI BLUE

MEDICI GREEN

FRENCH GRAY

ROSE BEIGE

POWDER GREEN

PALACE CREAM

CLOUD WHITE

POWDER PINK

APPLE GREEN

FRENCH LILAC

ORIENTAL GOLD

SEVRES BLUE

ROSE POMPADOUR

POMPADOUR BLUE

FRENCH TURQUOISE

DU BARRY RED

CHART 6 FOR CHAPTER 5

The colors of this chart cover the French periods of Louis XVI, Directoire and Empire. While a Classical revival occurred around 1774 —which changed the aspect of furniture, decoration and architecture—the pastels of Louis XV were maintained. Later, however, after about 1795, the deeper and fuller hues of Greece, Rome and the Renaissance were restored. Thereafter, French styles were repetitive.

FRENCH LOUIS XVI AND AFTER

CHALK GREEN

CHALK BEIGE

FLESH PINK

PALE CITRON

FRENCH ROSE

FRENCH GOLD

EMPIRE RED

EMPIRE YELLOW

EMPIRE GREEN

DEEP RUBY

AZURE BLUE

SALMON

AMETHYST

GRAY MAUVE

GRAY BLUE

PALE IVORY

CHART 7 FOR CHAPTER 6

Early English colors followed the Renaissance tradition in the Tudor, Elizabethan and Stuart periods. A break came with William and Mary or Queen Anne (1688-1727) during which English taste began to express itself. True individuality came with Early Georgian and the unique taste of Thomas Chippendale II. Note the preference for greens and for colors of fairly deep and rich tone. All the samples are authentic and taken from historical examples.

ENGLISH THROUGH EARLY GEORGIAN

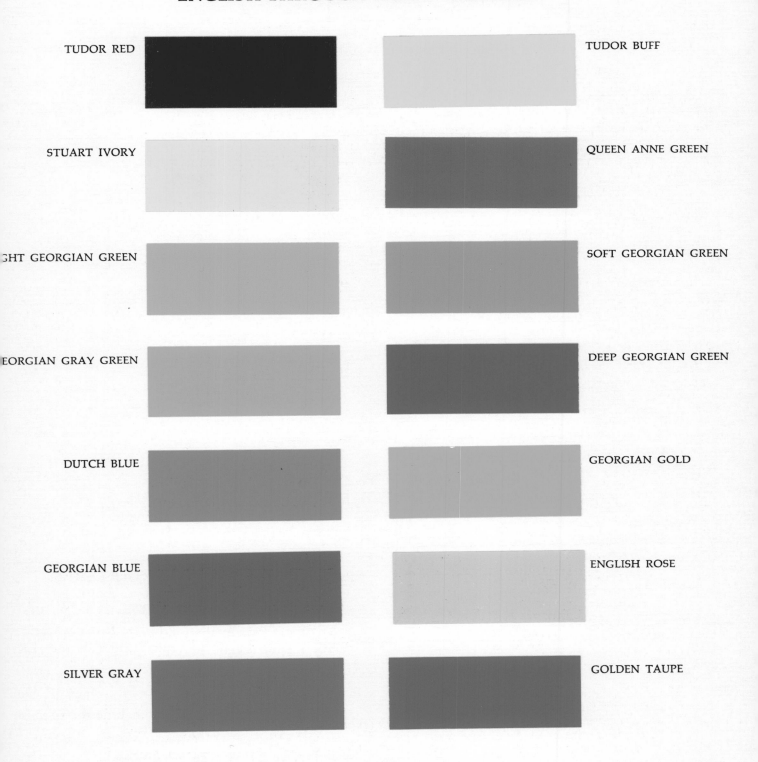

TUDOR RED

TUDOR BUFF

STUART IVORY

QUEEN ANNE GREEN

GHT GEORGIAN GREEN

SOFT GEORGIAN GREEN

EORGIAN GRAY GREEN

DEEP GEORGIAN GREEN

DUTCH BLUE

GEORGIAN GOLD

GEORGIAN BLUE

ENGLISH ROSE

SILVER GRAY

GOLDEN TAUPE

CHART 8 FOR CHAPTER 7

The Classical revival came to England around 1760 and was made notable by Robert Adam. Decorative styles became more symmetrical and formal. Adam colors were mostly pastels, as shown on the upper part of the chart. These are Late Georgian and they include the refined colors of Josiah Wedgwood. Then as happened in France (Directoire and Empire), English Regency revived the deeper and richer shade.

ENGLISH LATE GEORGIAN AND AFTER

LIGHT ADAM GREEN

DEEP ADAM GREEN

ADAM IVORY

ADAM YELLOW

ADAM GRAY

OPAL PINK

OPAL BLUE

OPAL GREEN

BRITISH GOLD

BRITISH BLUE

PALE GRECIAN BLUE

WEDGWOOD BLUE

GRECIAN LILAC

JASPER YELLOW

REGENCY RED

REGENCY BROWN

4 FRENCH DECORATION, UP THROUGH LOUIS XV

French interiors prior to the Renaissance were heavily Gothic, though with something of an Italian quality. Furniture was bulky and substantial, made of oak and only occasionally decorated with color. Walls were painted white or buff for the most part and many structural features of wood or stone were left exposed. Historically there were reasons for the French to be the first of other European countries to catch the spirit of the Italian Renaissance and to bring its manifestations onto French soil. While the Renaissance was in full flower in Italy the two countries were embroiled in power struggles; Louis XII, who reigned from 1498 to 1515, fought the Italians at Milan and Genoa but failed at Naples.

His successor, Francis I, one of the truly great kings of France (he reigned from 1515 to 1547), resumed the Italian wars and developed a respect for the great artists of Italy. To his court came such eminent Italian masters as da Vinci, Cellini, Andrea de Sarto, and one of the famous Della Robbias. There were craftsmen with Italian, German, Flemish, and Spanish backgrounds. Both Fontainebleau and the Louvre were begun. Bulky Gothic ornaments gave way to more delicate motifs, the laurel and acanthus, which planted the seeds of later Baroque and Rococo styles.

THE WELL-KNOWN HALL OF MIRRORS AT VERSAILLES WHICH TYPIFIES THE SUMPTUOUSNESS OF THE FRENCH PERIODS UP THROUGH LOUIS XV. RENAISSANCE INFLUENCE IS DOMINANT. PHOTOGRAPH COURTESY FRENCH GOVERNMENT TOURIST OFFICE.

Color at the time of Francis I, therefore, was clearly Renaissance (as on Chart 4, page 29). But French taste and an expression individual to French national temperament and culture would soon become evident and would lead to what may justifiably be called the most elegant of all eras in the history of western interior decoration.

France under Francis I saw the fullest development of the Renaissance spirit. Having been properly schooled, the Frenchman now could strike out and prove the high degree of his individuality.

Worth recording here, perhaps, and included on Chart 5 (page 31) are a few late French Renaissance colors. Note Medici Blue and Medici Green introduced, according to history, by Catherine de Medici, queen to Henry II who had followed Francis I. Taste began to

show the refinement and discrimination most persons associate with the French.

The Fontainebleau of Francis I and Henry IV is second only to Versailles in magnificence. These abodes of kings became national shrines and were refurbished and redecorated through passing generations. At Fontainebleau there was much use of French Gray, shown on Chart 5. It was applied as a foil for decorations which covered virtually all wall space. The palace today contains rooms that echo the taste of later kings and queens, including Marie Antoinette, Napoleon, and Josephine. There are old salons and chambers which later tenants refurnished. Fontainebleau in its own right is definitely Renaissance and has the lavish gilt of the sixteenth and seventeenth centuries.

The French style flourished and began to blossom. Louis XIII, during his reign from

1601 to 1643, started Versailles as a chateau and introduced parquet floors, rare woods, rich velvets and brocades—and more color.

Then Louis XIV, the Sun King, (reigning from 1643 to 1715) conquered the Renaissance and brought it under French domination, at least in his own country. Under him, Versailles was rebuilt and enlarged. The head of a vain and powerful France, Louis XIV made Versailles the envy of every living ruler of his day. The Baroque style with all its gilt, ornament, mirrors, tapestries, textiles, marbles, woods, paintings, and other decorations, reached its zenith. Many of the colors were strident—crimson, gold, green. There was a vogue for Oriental forms and hues.

Perhaps it can be said that the Louis XIV period, like the Renaissance, was still masculine. It tended to be heavy and bold in scale.

THE THRONE ROOM AT FONTAINEBLEAU. THE STYLE IS MOSTLY RENAISSANCE WITH MUCH USE OF LIGHT GRAY AND PALE CREAM COLORS OFFSET BY GILT IN RELIEF ORNAMENTS, MOLDINGS, DECORATIONS. PRACTICALLY ALL WALL SPACE WAS ADORNED. PHOTOGRAPH COURTESY WARE MEMORIAL LIBRARY, COLUMBIA UNIVERSITY.

In fact, patronage had come largely from men. French decoration would later come under the influence of women—queens and mistresses—and take on more refinement and restraint.

Chart 5 shows two commonly used colors of the Louis XIV style on the refined side, Rose Beige and Powder Green. The Powder Green in particular was used in large areas as a paint or stain over wood. It had a delicate beauty which the English later copied, took to their hearts, and used.

In preparing Chart 5 selectivity was imperative. Use of all the colors of the Renaissance would lead to a record looking like a complete atlas of the entire spectrum. What is remarkable about French decoration, notably the period of Louis XV, is the display of a taste different to any that had ever been expressed before. It is closer to modern preferences, for it introduces a new and refreshing subtlety of pastels and muted tones which glorify the Creative tradition and give it a more intimate, personal, and cultured sophistication. In fact, it becomes soft-spoken, affectionate, seductive, and feminine.

French decoration went from the Baroque to the Rococo during the reign of Louis XV (1715-1774). The entry was through what is known as the Regency period during which Philippe d'Orleans handled the affairs of the youthful monarch. There was a quick transition from that which was massive and square to that which became more curvilinear, softer, and freer—with many influences from the Chinese. This then shifted to florid pretensions and to absurd mannerisms and sentimentality (which needed a return to the Classicism of Louis XVI, Directoire, and Empire to bring back to its senses).

It is a curious phenomenon of the reign of Louis XV that it also marked a time in western philosophy and thought known as the Age of Enlightenment. While a decadent court gave itself to continuous pageantry and dissipation, men like Voltaire and Rousseau (and Paine and Jefferson in America), wrote of democracy and new freedom for men. France, however, surrendered its resources to its royal court and saw the rise of the upper bourgeoisie. The time was one of self-indulgence and extravagance.

But it was a glorious era for color. Where formerly social life was conducted in big spaces

GRAND SALON AT THE CHATEAU DE DAMPIERRE. HERE IS THE ROCOCO STYLE CARRIED TO EXTREMES—ELABORATE, INTRICATE, YET IN CONSISTENTLY GOOD, IF DECADENT, TASTE. PHOTOGRAPH COURTESY JACQUES BODART, INC.

and large salons there were now smaller apartments and boudoirs. If any one thing is typical of the period it is the chaise-longue. Though the trenchant color might be suitable for the grand interiors, it was too impulsive for the smaller parlor, sitting room, or chamber. And so the art of interior decoration saw its truly first and tasteful application of the delicate tint and refined shade or tone.

Dominant here were the superior taste and influence of Madame de Pompadour, mistress of Louis XV for nearly twenty years. Intelligent, literate, musical, political, she was very much in control and stood at the head of all court functions and intrigues.

It was Madame de Pompadour who patronized the great French painters of the day—(Boucher, Fragonard, Watteau, Greuze), made Chinese art (Chinoiserie) popular, founded the Sevres porcelain industry, and supported Aubusson tapestries and carpets. Her wellsprings for color came from these remarkable sources, feminized the art of decoration, and undoubtedly put her name down in history (at least, in this author's book) as the most original, talented, and perceptive patron of color since the time of the Renaissance. This lady's taste, intimate and personal as it was—and well suited to informal modes of life—has blossomed and reblossomed ever since. There probably have been no unique or distinct color styles since those of Madame de Pompadour, for it would be difficult to create a "feeling"

for color which she did not at one time sense and exploit. The world has copied her right and left, so to speak, ever since.

Refer now to Chart 5 (page 31). Palace Cream and Cloud White, like Powder Green, were common ground colors of the Louis XV period, usually with the widespread accompaniment of gilt. New to the art of decoration, and not seen on the previous charts of this book, are the pastels and lush tones of Powder Pink, Apple Green, French Lilac, Oriental Gold, Sevres Blue, Rose Pompadour, Pompadour Blue, and French Turquoise. Here are the styles which will appear in later decades.

These appealing colors are quite French in character. They were applied to smaller apartments and accompanied by elegant furniture and accessories. A great deal of furniture was painted or gilded. There was much inlay work in wood, marble, porcelain, hand-painted china, and metal. Textile and upholstery were florid. One might assume from these interiors that life was a never-ending series of games, flirtations, dinners, parties, romps in gardens and woodlands.

Madame Du Barry, who succeeded Madame de Pompadour, is given her own color—Du Barry Red. This mistress of Louis XV unfortunately came upon bad times after the death of the king in 1774 and was later guillotined.

Although the form, shape, and plastic character of the Louis XV period was shortly revolutionized, the colors persisted.

5 FRENCH DECORATION, LOUIS XVI AND AFTER

By the late eighteenth century French politics stood in dire need of a revolution. The French court had drained the national treasury and gone into debt—amongst other causatory items was costly intervention in the struggle between America and England. Besides, economic conditions had changed. Nobility was being replaced by an upper bourgeoisie which was making fortunes in industry and trade. This prosperity, however, was not shared with the multitude. July 14, 1789, Bastille Day, was in the offing. Some credit should be given to Louis XVI (he reigned between 1774-1792) for trying to institute reforms, to practice personal economy, and to appoint upright ministers. In this he was quite opposed by his court and by the frivolities and extravagances of his wife, Marie Antoinette.

Revolution was brewing on all sides, although that which took place in interior design and architecture had nothing whatsoever to do with politics. The sharp break that occurred between the Louis XV and Louis XVI decorative styles, which also occurred in England and America, may perhaps be traced to the direct or indirect influence of a German, one Johann

Winckelmann, who has already been mentioned in this book. Although Greek and Roman excavations had been going on for some years, it was Winckelmann who truly founded the modern science of archaeology.

Of humble birth, a cobbler's son, Winckelmann was obsessed by a desire to dig into the ruins of antiquity. After a fabulous career (well worth the reader's time to look up), he began to publish, between 1762-1767, a series of monumental works on Pompeii and Herculaneum. They immediately astonished and fascinated the world of architecture and decoration and caused the most abrupt change ever encountered in the history of these subjects. The break had something of the impact of an ax. (For example, let an American compare the Governor's Palace at Williamsburg with Jefferson's Monticello, the one Georgian, and the other a simulated Greek temple.)

France at the time of Louis XVI went all out, so to speak, for Greece, Rome, and Herr Winckelmann. The feeling went mathematical and symmetrical, with straight lines rather than curved ones. Although there was plenty of ornamentation, the spirit was Classical.

In matters of color, however, there was serious conflict. There were some who, like the great painter, David, insisted on the pure, formal colors of the Greek and Roman tradition. This was consistent, at least, and was respected in the Directoire and Empire styles that followed. Yet French taste was under feminine domination. Mmes. Pompadour and Du Barry had influenced Louis XV. Now Marie Antoinette, with equal taste, would influence the reign of Louis XVI.

In consequence (and the same is true of England), the Classical tradition set fashions in forms, shapes, and patterns, but the Creative tradition held out in favor of delicate and refined colors unknown to ancient times.

If some purists wanted the formal—and authentic—color to complement the Classical revival, French fashion would have little of it.

The feeling for color, therefore, held to the pastel and muted tone and was not greatly unlike that of the period of Louis XV, despite the fact that furniture, interior, and decorative styles were quite different.

Marie Antoinette, a woman of luxury, is said to have preferred the gentle touch. She also favored the smaller room as an escape from the stiff grandeur of the court salons. Once again this came close to modern conceptions, and the colors of the period—like those of the Classical revival in England—still are repeated in countless homes of Europe, Great Britain, and America.

If anything, Marie Antoinette's taste was even more subtle than that of Madame de Pompadour. A few of her preferred tints are shown at the top of Chart 6 (page 33): Chalk Green, Chalk Beige, Flesh Pink, Pale Citron,

PRIVATE ROOMS LIKE THIS FRENCH BOUDOIR OF THE PERIOD OF LOUIS XVI WERE BUILT AT FONTAINEBLEAU, VERSAILLES, AND PETIT TRIANON. PALE TINTS OF GREEN, BEIGE, PINK, YELLOW—FAVORITES OF MARIE ANTOINETTE—WERE USED. PHOTOGRAPH COURTESY THORNE EUROPEAN ROOMS IN MINIATURE, THE ART INSTITUTE OF CHICAGO.

CLASSICISM PREVAILED IN THE DESIGN OF THE FRENCH DIRECTOIRE AND CONSULATE PERIODS AS CAN BE SEEN IN THIS BEDROOM AND BOUDOIR. HOWEVER, COLORS WENT STRONGER, AND SYMBOLS OF REVOLUTION APPEARED. NOTE POMPEIIAN TOUCHES. PHOTOGRAPH THORNE EUROPEAN ROOMS IN MINIATURE, THE ART INSTITUTE OF CHICAGO.

HERE IS FRENCH EMPIRE IN FULL DETAIL; GRAND SALON, CHATEAU DE GRAND-VAUX. NOTE DECORATIVE BORROWINGS FROM GREECE, ROME, EGYPT. THE SILK WALL PANELS ARE VIVID GREEN. UPHOLSTERY AND CARPET ARE IN RICH HUES. PHOTOGRAPH COURTESY JACQUES BODART, INC.

THIS IS A SALON OF THE FRENCH EMPIRE PERIOD, ABOUT 1810, WHILE NAPOLEON WAS IN POWER. THERE IS RATHER STIFF FORMALITY, ROMAN AND EGYPTIAN MOTIFS, GENUINE AND IMITATION MARBLE. STRONG COLORS ARE SEEN IN UPHOLSTERY, DRAPERY, CARPETING, SUCH AS RED, GOLD, BROWN, DEEP BLUE, AND EMERALD GREEN. PHOTOGRAPH COURTESY THORNE EUROPEAN ROOMS IN MINIATURE, THE ART INSTITUTE OF CHICAGO.

French Rose, French Gold. One recognizes similarities to the preceding period of Louis XV, but it should not be forgotten that, as mentioned, the whole concept of *design* broke with the Rococo and returned to Classical ideals. Color was really the only thing that was held over from the previous era. But now color, too, would undergo revolution.

Louis XVI and Marie Antoinette reigned from 1774 to 1792. They were driven from the court in 1792 and guillotined in 1793. The light touch in color went out with them—for a while, at least—was temporarily restored by Napoleon's Josephine, and then finally flourished in a more distant future where it still respectably endures.

Following Louis XVI came the Directoire and Consulate Periods which persisted until 1804. Even more that was simple, graceful, and direct was produced in the decorative arts.

A wealthy class still had money to spend and could continue to express the best of French taste. Colors, however, like the patriotic fervor of the times, went strong. Symbols of the French Revolution appeared—Phrygian caps, arrows, pikes, wreaths, stars, plus the full red, white, and blue of the tricolor of France.

With Napoleon and Empire (1804-1815), the revolution went on. Decorative designs, richly and deeply colored, were taken directly from Greece, Rome, and Egypt, lands quite familiar to the conquering Frenchman. There was absolute symmetry, geometric shape, heavy proportion. Many things looked like archaeological findings out of the past. Napoleon designed symbols of his own which included the sphinx, the bee, and the letter N surrounded by a laurel wreath. There were lions and griffins and caryatids. Walls, fabrics, furnishings were full and intense.

Several Directoire and Empire colors are shown on Chart 6: Empire Red, Empire Yellow, and Empire Green which Napoleon favored (along with white and gold). Also typical of the two periods are Deep Ruby, Azure Blue, Salmon, Amethyst. While there is some refinement in these latter four, they still are several shades down from the delicate pastels of Madame de Pompadour.

Napoleon, however, didn't have his way throughout. He was wed to an Empress, Josephine, who had a taste for extravagance like that of Marie Antoinette. Besides, he was often away on campaigns, and while he wrote her impassioned letters — which she rarely answered—Josephine brought into the mighty Empire style the genteel taste of some of her royal predecessors. According to record, Josephine liked grayed and muted colors which reflected glints of blue, silver, mauve, gold, or pink. Three of these are shown on Chart 6: Gray Mauve, Gray Blue, and Pale Ivory. With them the circle goes more or less full round to Louis XV, but even more quietly.

This is the French story of color, one that is not likely to be forgotten in the future history of the decorative arts. Much of it was emulated in England and in America—not to mention other western countries. Here perhaps was one of the brightest and most original eras of all. Here was delicacy without timidity, sophistication without self-conscious pretense, and an emotionalism which only the most sensitive culture (decadent or not) could be expected to achieve.

Finally, a note on early nineteenth century Biedermeier. After the Napoleonic wars and the French Revolution, the independent states of Germany—from about 1820 to 1840—developed a middle-class style of decorative arts. This was in reaction to the pompous formality of French Empire. The so-called man in the street could hardly afford the ostentations of emperors and nobles. So in the caricature of an imaginary Papa Biedermeier, a whole range of everyday possessions was humorously portrayed. Biedermeier furniture and decoration, however, were by no means imaginary. French vanity was brought down to earth by the more practical Germans, and much that was simple, charming, and graceful was created.

The Biedermeier style, once subject to ridicule, later had its better elements accepted and recognized as of high artistic quality. Color was generously used, with emphasis on greens, blues and browns. Blond wood tones prevailed in furniture. Yet if the "period" had a long and successful reign in parts of Europe, little of it came to America, for here the English tradition became firmly entrenched.

6 ENGLISH DECORATION, UP THROUGH EARLY GEORGIAN

The British temperament is by no means that of the French. The one is deliberate and practical, and the other quite temperamental. If one were to pick a typical French color, it would be rose. For the English—at least in the Early Georgian period—the color would be green. Green, of course, is a natural-looking hue. Despite prejudices (often of a religious sort) against green by the Protestant Britisher, this color has been used by him more freely and often than any other, and the tradition was carried over to America.

If French taste is to be credited with vivacity and innovation, English taste shows remarkable discrimination and reserve. The French have tended to be outgoing and somewhat pretentious, like the Italians, whereas the English have taken fashion probably more to mind than to heart. While French colors suggest a lively social environment with a lot going on, English colors suggest a more home-like and comfortable setting in which cultural interests will be intellectual rather than sensual.

In the Stuart period (1603-1688) which includes Jacobean, Commonwealth, and Restoration, the Renaissance in England reached full bloom. Architects with the taste of Inigo Jones and Sir Christopher Wren introduced Greek and Roman revivals. There were more Italian workers, while religious freedom attracted French, Flemish, German, and Dutch craftsmen. Yet the decorative feeling was still massive, solid, and ornate. There were more silks, damasks, velvets, brocades, leathers in brilliant hues—plus a new art of lacquering. The colors, however, were still Renaissance and similar to those shown on Chart 4 (page 29). Where painted, most walls were still white or buff.

With the William and Mary, or Queen Anne, period came a more abrupt break which extended from about 1688 to 1727. King William, in fact, of Dutch origin, did not think much of English taste and set out to change it. Walnut was introduced as a decorative wood and was sometimes bleached. In furniture and decoration that which had been straight and heavy became curved and convex. Furniture was painted and lacquered, at times in imitation of marble. There was the beginning of an individual English style and feeling, one that was sleek and sophisticated. Chinese wallpaper and porcelain became popular. While there was not much attention to painted walls (decorations were preferred), green was introduced and became the favored color note of the Early Georgian period that immediately followed.

With the Early Georgian style (from 1727 to about 1760), the British really hit their stride. Perhaps no period in all English history is more beautiful, unique, friendly, warm, and intimate than the Georgian. It became the rage in America and is still held in reverence.

British economy had much to do with this. Up to the eighteenth century there had been strong kings, weak kings, rebels, religious and civil wars. Now there was more diffuse wealth, prosperity in industry and trade. There were more people with more money, and this demanded a certain gracious and luxurious home life. Taste that had flowed into England from Italy, France, the Netherlands, from far-off China, and India, was fused into a definite British style having British quality. The nation had put its talented wits together and entered the finest decorative era in its history.

Maybe climate has something to do with all this. Where there is less sunlight, there is likely to be restraint in the use of color. And the people who live in colder, foggier, and wetter lands are likely to be sober and diligent: the struggle for shelter and security requires greater attention and effort; the home is truly a sanctuary and retreat, and its beauty must be appropriate to its utility.

The history of English period styles in color requires little telling prior to the Tudor-Elizabethan era (approximately 1509 to 1603). This marked the end of the medieval and Gothic and the beginning of the Renaissance.

The English take justifiable pride in King Hal and Queen Bess. A lot went on during their reigns—in religious and political upheaval, exploration and colonization, literature, drama, philosophy. Life, however, still clung to medieval precedents. It would take civil war and Puritan revolt to stop Henry VIII from hanging two thousand men a year for theft (Elizabeth reduced the mortality rate to about four hundred per annum) and begin to spread the benefits of national prosperity over a wider social front. The great medieval hall in which the privileged ate, danced, sang, and often slept would give way to a more ordered and compartmental existence.

Tudor and Elizabethan furniture and decoration were huge, solid, bulky. Walls were mostly oak, stone, brick, and heavy with tapestries. White and buff are perhaps the only colors to be mentioned and may be recalled by the reader in his memory of half-timbered Elizabethan structures.

The Renaissance moved in swiftly and with the immigration came skilled workers from Italy who pretty well disposed of the old Gothic spirit.

Where once kings, princes, and their mistresses had guided fashion, now it was a wealthy class supporting a series of eminent cabinetmakers and decorators. Foremost among them was Thomas Chippendale II, one of three bearing the famous name. In 1754, he published *The Gentleman and Cabinet-Maker's Directory* which had phenomenal sale and distribution, was the first of many prototypes, and was so wholeheartedly accepted that it set the pattern of English furniture and decoration as if by national law. Seldom has the work of one man been so suddenly and generously adopted.

Thomas Chippendale was quite a genius. A great admirer of both the Louis XIV and Louis XV periods, he did not just take what was good from these sources, he amalgamated them along with what he admired from the Italian,

THE GREAT HALL OF AN ENGLISH TUDOR MANSION WHERE JUST ABOUT ALL THE FUNCTIONS OF A HOME WERE FOUND IN ONE AREA. THIS IS LATE SIXTEENTH CENTURY AND SHOWS GOTHIC AND RENAISSANCE INFLUENCES. WOODWORK IS OAK, WITH UPPER WALLS A LIGHT BUFF. PHOTOGRAPH COURTESY THORNE EUROPEAN ROOMS IN MINIATURE, THE ART INSTITUTE OF CHICAGO.

IN THIS ENGLISH SALON OF THE STUART PERIOD, EARLY SEVENTEENTH CENTURY, DECORATIONS WERE INFLUENCED BY ITALIAN RENAISSANCE AND LOST THE HEAVINESS OF MEDIEVAL TIMES. THERE ARE BROCADED WALLS, DECORATED CEILINGS, WHITE OR GILDED DADOES AND CORNICES. PHOTOGRAPH COURTESY THORNE EUROPEAN ROOMS IN MINIATURE, THE ART INSTITUTE OF CHICAGO.

Gothic, and Chinese. His was an eclectic talent that founded an enduring "school." There would be Chinese Chippendale, Scottish Chippendale, Irish Chippendale—even Philadelphia Chippendale—as time went on and his imitators became legion.

Chippendale introduced mahogany as a decorative wood—along with a rich interpretation of other national cultures. There are beautiful furniture pieces, textiles, carpets, mirrors, wallpapers which represent a sort of universal beauty, surprisingly varied, but all with a dominant and consistent English flavor. He was the father of the entire style of the Middle Georgian period. What he designed looked English and was English. Products of his creation swept across his own land and made quite a conquest in America despite political troubles with the American colonies. A third generation (Thomas III) made furniture for the Brothers Adam and thus extended the heritage of a talented father and grandfather into the Late Georgian period.

Not many people these days live in Elizabethan or Stuart homes. Nor are the red brick mansions of Queen Anne's day very often seen. However, the Georgian house with its Chippendale furnishings, ceiling and wall decorations, and painted wood paneling, remains the pride of England and America, preserved in countless restorations and repeated again and again in modern architectural adaptations.

The colors of Chart 7 (page 35) are mostly those of the Early Georgian period. The top four, however, cover the Tudor and Stuart periods. As has been mentioned, wall painting other than white was virtually unknown. Many of the materials used were natural wood, stone, or brick. For decorative purposes these spaces were heavy with tapestries or covered with brocade. And the colors thereon (as well as on decorated furniture) were those of the Renaissance shown on Chart 4.

Tudor Red, Chart 7, was a typical textile wall covering. Tudor Buff and Stuart Ivory were employed as occasional wall finishes, often over a rough plaster.

Queen Anne Green introduced a new feeling and led to the Early Georgian style. It had quite a vogue as a paint or stain over wood paneling—mostly during the epoch of Thomas Chippendale II when Britain had broken with

GRACIOUSNESS IN HOME INTERIOR STYLING CAME WITH THE SO-CALLED QUEEN ANNE PERIOD. HERE IS AN EXCELLENT EXAMPLE, THOUGH AN AMERICAN ONE (1733). WALLS ARE OFF-WHITE, UP-HOLSTERED FURNITURE GOLD, DRAPERIES GREEN. PHOTOGRAPH COURTESY HENRY FRANCIS DU PONT WINTERTHUR MUSEUM.

WITH THE CEILING FIXTURE OMITTED, HERE IS THE KITCHEN OF SULGRAVE MANOR, THE LATER ENGLISH HOME OF THE WASHINGTON FAMILY, ABOUT 1700. IT IS PRACTICAL, PROVINCIAL AND DATES TO THE TIME OF QUEEN ANNE WHEN THE UNIQUELY LIVABLE QUALITY OF ENGLISH INTERIOR DESIGN BEGAN TO EXPRESS ITSELF. PHOTOGRAPH COURTESY ENGLISH LIFE AND ANTIQUES MAGAZINE.

WHERE THE GEORGIAN STYLE BECOMES "FRIENDLY," AS WITH THE
FURNITURE AND CABINET WORK OF THOMAS CHIPPENDALE II, IT
RANKS AS ONE OF THE MOST MAGNIFICENT ERAS IN THE ENTIRE
HISTORY OF INTERIOR DESIGN. IN THIS "CHINESE-CHIPPENDALE"
BEDROOM, COLORS ARE DELICATE, THE DESIGN CONCEPT GRACE-
FUL AND WHIMSICAL. PHOTOGRAPH COURTESY THORNE EURO-
PEAN ROOMS IN MINIATURE, THE ART INSTITUTE OF CHICAGO.

HERE IS ANOTHER QUEEN ANNE IMPORT TO AMERICA, THIS FROM
A HOME IN DERRY, NEW HAMPSHIRE. WALLS ARE A MEDIUM
GREEN WHICH IS TYPICAL OF BOTH THE QUEEN ANNE AND GEOR-
GIAN PERIODS. PHOTOGRAPH COURTESY HENRY FRANCIS DU PONT
WINTERTHUR MUSEUM.

Italian, French, and Gothic influences.

Now to the Georgian colors which number ten on Chart 7. Bear the following observations in mind:

Georgian colors were chiefly on the medium or deep side. Late Georgian would refine them into lighter pastels.

Painted wood (pine) paneling was in fashion and often seen in tones of green, blue, and warm tan.

White, which was so abundantly used in America in Colonial times (with painted woodwork) was not altogether British in character. White would come in later. One may assume that while the British had Chinese or scenic wallpaper or textiles, the more frugal American left upper walls a plain white.

Curiously, there was little use of yellow which became popular in the American Colonies. However, there was considerable use of opaque gold (Georgian Gold on the chart).

Chart 7 shows five greens (including Queen Anne Green): Light Georgian Green, Soft Georgian Green, Georgian Gray Green, and Deep Georgian Green. All are authentic, and allowance could be made for in-between variations. As has been said, green is by all odds the most typically Early Georgian color.

Dutch Blue and Georgian Blue, both medium-deep in tone, are also in good tradition, as are Georgian Gold and English Rose. Note the softness of the latter color as compared with the bright pink and rose shades of the French.

Silver Gray and Golden Taupe are as well on the muted side. Indeed, the differing taste of Englishmen and Frenchmen can be seen at a glance by comparing Chart 7 with Charts 5 and 6. If the French demonstrated a blithe and vivacious taste, the English proved they had an eye for exquisite refinement.

HERE IS A FORMAL EXAMPLE OF EARLY GEORGIAN INTERIOR STYLING FROM A MANSION AT KIRTLINGTON PARK, OXFORDSHIRE. WALLS ARE OFF-WHITE. PHOTOGRAPH COURTESY THE METROPOLITAN MUSEUM OF ART, FLETCHER FUND, 1932.

7 ENGLISH DECORATION, LATE GEORGIAN AND AFTER

The entire magnificent era of English furniture design and decoration—from Chippendale through Adam, Hepplewhite, Sheraton to Regency—is known as the Georgian. As happened in France, however, there was a sudden change in the midst of all this creative effort, due in large part to the archaeological findings and writings of Johann Winckelmann on Pompeii and Herculaneum.

And as in France, while there was an inspired revival of Classical forms, shapes, and designs, the colors went pastel as they did at the time of Louis XVI—only to go temporarily deep again with English Regency and its corresponding French Directoire and Empire. (In America, the same break occurred between the Georgian-Colonial tradition and the Federal. Williamsburg, for example, is Early Georgian, while Mount Vernon is Late Georgian.)

Edwin Foley in his competent work, *The Book of Decorative Furniture*, says of the eighteenth century: "A well-educated English gentleman may be truly said to be of no country whatever; he talks and dresses French, he rivals the Spaniard in indolence and the German in drinking; his house is Grecian, his offices Gothic, and his furniture Chinese."

Period styles as a rule are eclectic. What of human culture is not? Chippendale was able to create an individual British "school" which differed from that of other countries even though it borrowed from them.

Late Georgian really means the Brothers Adam. Scottish by birth and architects by training, they revolutionized the decorative arts of England. Robert Adam, the best known, visited Italy, was imbued with the Classical spirit, and returned to London to be elected a

Fellow of the Royal Society and appointed architect to the King and Queen. He was at one time (1768) a member of Parliament. A partnership with his brother, James, became known as the Adelphi.

Unlike any other talented designer in his country, Robert Adam had the skill and ability of an architect and concerned himself not alone with furniture design but with everything that went into a home—room shapes and proportions, panelling, ornamentation, sculpture, textiles, wallpaper, accessories.

These were fertile days for his genius. Great Britain was exceedingly prosperous and had colonized Canada and India, although it lost Colonial America. The nobility was flush with money and so was a wealthy class of business men, merchants, and traders. A romantic movement in art flourished, and science and

MOUNT VERNON, WHICH WASHINGTON ACQUIRED IN 1754 AND
WHICH HE SUBSEQUENTLY IMPROVED, MAY BE CONSIDERED LATE
GEORGIAN. THE SQUARE COLUMNS OF THE PIAZZA WERE ERECTED
IN 1777 AND REFLECT THE CLASSICAL REVIVAL OF THE LATE
EIGHTEENTH CENTURY. PHOTOGRAPH COURTESY THE MOUNT
VERNON LADIES' ASSOCIATION.

THIS IS AN ADAM DINING ROOM FROM LANDSDOWNE HOUSE,
LONDON, CA. 1765-68. THE CLASSICAL REVIVAL SEPARATES THE
EARLY AND LATE GEORGIAN PERIODS. LARGELY UNDER THE IN-
FLUENCE OF THE BROTHERS ADAM, THE MORE GENTEEL STYLE
OF CHIPPENDALE BECOMES FORMALIZED, WITH GRECIAN AND
ROMAN DETAILS. IN THIS INTERIOR, THE WALLS ARE A PALE GRAY
AND THE TRIM OFF-WHITE. PHOTOGRAPH COURTESY THE MET-
ROPOLITAN MUSEUM OF ART, ROGERS FUND, 1932.

industry prospered.

What Robert Adam had to offer became dominant in the interior arts with amazing speed. His introduction of Classical motifs was ahead of the French by almost a decade. He later became engrossed by the Louis XVI style —which he had anticipated and no doubt influenced—and published some of his books of designs with English and French texts.

Adam was a great innovator. All of his designs were formal, refined, classically pure and true—and perhaps "dry" for all this. If Early Georgian had a livable and home-like quality, Adam Georgian took on certain of the stiff elements of a museum. One could sit around at ease in the environment of Mr. Chippendale, but with Mr. Adam one needed to be fully dressed, reserved in speech and erect in posture. And nothing in the Adam interior was to be disturbed!

Adam furniture was quite beautiful in its simple elegance, symmetry, fineness, and squareness. He brought fame to the sideboard with its silver service. His furniture showed restraint and deliberation. There were lighter woods, such as satinwood, much inlay work, slender and delicate ornament. Many home items were gilded. Carving gave way to inlaid and painted designs having cream, pale green, white, or even black grounds. Where the designs were painted, the colors used were also pastel. Nothing was to be officious, aggressive, or pretentious. Oval rooms and rectangular rooms were decorated in pale tints, using paint or silk. There was much evidence of Greek

ROBERT ADAM DOMINATED THE LATE GEORGIAN PERIOD. HE GAVE UP WOOD PANELING AND WALLPAPER FOR PAINT AND PLASTER. EXCAVATIONS AT POMPEII WERE RESPONSIBLE FOR THIS SUDDEN TURN OF ENGLISH TASTE. THE ADAM STYLE, HOWEVER, TENDS TO STIFFNESS AND DRYNESS. PASTEL COLORS ARE HIGHLY PREFERRED. PHOTOGRAPH COURTESY THORNE EUROPEAN ROOMS IN MINIATURE, THE ART INSTITUTE OF CHICAGO.

sculpture and ornament—the acanthus leaf and honeysuckle, laurel garlands, fluting, scrolls, urns, and the like.

From Early Georgian to Late Georgian, while *design* went formal and classical, *colors* kept moving up into pastels. These pastels will look quite familiar to modern Americans, for they have remained in or just out of fashion ever since. Robert Adam was wise to use these pale tints, for his Classical forms had the light touch which made the two compatible.

There was a decline in the popularity of greens. No longer did they crowd out the rest of the spectrum. With Adam came opal tints, with an occasional deep tone. However, lightness of color was the rule, while depth of color was the exception.

In perfect harmony with the classicism of Adam was the pottery of Josiah Wedgwood. Grecian ceramic panels or insets were often introduced into cabinets. Wedgwood developed light and deep blue, lilac, and he also used certain Jasper (quartz) colors in red, yellow, green, and brown.

Hepplewhite (he also made furniture for the Brothers Adam) got away from cold angu-

THOMAS SHERATON, LIKE HEPPLEWHITE, APPRECIATED THE BEAUTY OF FRENCH INTERIOR DESIGN. HIS INFLUENCE OVER THE LATE GEORGIAN PERIOD LED TO "COMFORTABLE" INTERIORS, SUCH AS SHOWN HERE IN WHICH PALE COLORS WERE DOMINANT. PHOTOGRAPH COURTESY THORNE EUROPEAN ROOMS IN MINIA-TURE, THE ART INSTITUTE OF CHICAGO.

THIS ROTUNDA AND LIBRARY ARE IN ENGLISH REGENCY, THE STYLE WHICH BROUGHT THE EMINENT GEORGIAN PERIOD TO AN ABRUPT END. AS HAPPENED AT THE SAME TIME IN FRANCE, INTE-RIOR STYLING BECAME GROTESQUE AND "ARCHAEOLOGICAL." COLORS SUDDENLY WENT FROM DELICATE PASTELS TO DEEP REDS, GREENS, BROWNS. PHOTOGRAPH COURTESY THORNE EUROPEAN ROOMS IN MINIATURE, THE ART INSTITUTE OF CHICAGO.

larity in his designs. He favored carved mahogany, inlaid woods, painted and japanned surfaces. While his furniture became more famous than that of Adam, one does not associate it with such precise interior styling. The same is true of the work of Shearer, "the apostle of simplicity." Chippendale and Hepplewhite furniture is still very much in evidence in traditional British home styles.

Thomas Sheraton, who followed Chippendale by some forty years, was still another master of the English cabinet-making industry. Sheraton's taste came close to modern taste. Although he produced great variety, he liked the graceful form. He became a Baptist and wrote on theology as well as furniture; perhaps this religious fervor developed an inner spirit which made him sensitive to the neat and subtle. He also went in for inventions, such as folding tables and ladders, disappearing drawers, secret compartments. Like Adam, he preferred wood inlay and painted decoration to relief carving.

While Hepplewhite and Sheraton designed and produced beautiful furniture, they contributed little to the story of color in the Late

Georgian period. Changes in taste for color go from Chippendale to Adam and thence to English Regency, named for The Prince of Wales who later became George IV. An ill-tempered man with extravagant taste, and something of a libertine according to history, his preference was for the exotic and excessive. During his reign English taste was brought downhill as if in a gilded Roman chariot.

With English Regency, the reign of Robert Adam declines. As happened in French Directoire and Empire—and at the same time—English individuality gave way to a cold and literal archaeology. The Regency style became grotesque, coarse, and inept. There were Roman couches, bookcases, and cabinets with the facades of ancient temples, stiff elements from Egypt. Besides, the machine age began to take over from the hand craftsman. As to colors, they went dark and heavy as they did in France —deep reds, greens, browns (two are shown in Chart 8 on page 37). A perfect example of the English Regency style will be found at the Royal Pavilion in Brighton which is now a museum.

After this, the glory of England settled down to an amalgamation of all the greatness it had created up through the early nineteenth century. There would be nothing much more to talk about until the singular reign of Queen Victoria which began in 1837.

In retrospect, most Americans and many Britishers tend to group the taste of Chippendale, Adam, Hepplewhite, and Sheraton into one venerable eighteenth century period. In fact, the cabinetmakers of the time did the same thing themselves in their catalogs and writings. Yet in color, Early Georgian (Chart 7) shows richness, depth, and refinement. Late Georgian (Chart 8) shows a progression to light and delicate pastels. Regency shows a rebound —merely temporary—to classical starkness.

As to English "feeling," Americans appear to hold reverence for Early Georgian modes of architecture and Late Georgian colors at one and the same time. This will be evident in the discussions of the next chapter.

To review the colors of Chart 8, note their refinement as against those of Louis XVI (Chart 6) of roughly the same chronology. English taste has developed, and its spirit is akin to that expressed in America in the late eighteenth century. Adam colors for the most part are at the top of Chart 8: Light Adam Green and Deep Adam Green, Adam Ivory, Adam Yellow, Adam Gray, Opal Pink, Opal Blue, Opal Green. The two deeper tones, British Gold and British Blue, are more reminiscent of the Early Georgian period and were effectively used in formal interiors.

Wedgwood colors are found in Pale Grecian Blue, Wedgwood Blue, Grecian Lilac, and Jasper Yellow.

Of several English Regency colors, two are shown: Regency Red and Regency Brown. (Empire Green of Chart 6 could be included for England as well.)

Colors of the Early and Late Georgian periods, plus several others of unique character, were repeated in America.

8 AMERICAN PERIOD STYLES

There are a number of unique aspects to the story of color and decoration in America. First of all, there is little to report before the middle of the seventeenth century—and this is a late start as far as history goes. Early settlers brought virtually nothing with them. Once landed, they were too busy seeking food and shelter to indulge themselves in much more than log cabins or mud huts.

Then too, settlements were scattered: the English in New England and Virginia, Dutch in New Amsterdam, Swedish in Delaware, German in Pennsylvania, French in Canada and New Orleans, Spanish in Florida, New Mexico, and California.

It was a primitive start with no palaces or chateaux to build or emulate. Architecture began with the simple home, church, and meeting hall. For quite a while most tools, utensils, and furniture were hand made, as were cloths and textiles. Thus the Renaissance, which had such a pronounced influence in Italy, France, and England, skipped America almost completely. The true beginning was little more than a survival of the Middle Ages and Gothic, and quite humble.

Because the American tradition was so strongly influenced by the British, the development of a decorative style constantly reflected that which was English. Much was done from memory. The Pilgrims of New England no doubt recalled the Elizabethan cottages of their birth, while the settlers of Virginia had visions of British architecture, antedating the Georgian.

For functional reasons, however, need was

often more significant than desire. Climates were different. There was little time to waste. Many a settler had to build his own edifice. Others had to employ pensioners or laborers, mostly unskilled. Quite important, lumber was everywhere and free to use. As a result, while English taste was commonly expressed, the American colonist very promptly showed skill and originality in adapting it to his materials and the special demands of his environment. The Cape Cod cottage and salt box home are cases in point. The plantations in Virginia, built on a larger scale and for a different mode of economic life, were more directly British.

So it was that the New England Early Colonial style consisted of timber homes with clay-filled and whitewashed walls—with the fireplace the center of all. The furniture was likely to be Jacobean. Most woodwork, oak and pine, was left unpainted. There were some wall hangings, needlework, pewter. The Pennsylvania-Germans, however, used color freely and developed the arts of pottery and glass.

With progress made and the eighteenth century under way, the American Colonial home took beautiful and liveable shape. Walnut became popular as a wood. There was more money to spend. The styles of William and Mary and Queen Anne were introduced. Walls were paneled, and wood trimmings, carved pilasters, and moldings came into use. This promptly led to a reverence for English Early Georgian and for the taste of Thomas Chippendale. Colors soon became rich and full.

Early Georgian, which is so beautifully preserved at Williamsburg, brought glory to the Colonies, and with it wealth and culture. Furniture and furnishings became quite elegant.

Walls and woodwork were painted, sometimes in one solid color, sometimes in two different hues. The tones were similar to those shown on Chart 7 devoted to English Early Georgian and a few are shown on Chart 9 (page 103) devoted to American. There were different shades of green, soft red, blue, gold, yellow, tan, gray. The Early Georgian manner in America was quite English, for the American colonist was still a loyal, if increasingly disturbed, subject. It was a generation of elegance. Craftsmen on the western side of the Atlantic gained eminence in all the decorative arts. Imports were no longer essential. A certain independence took shape and was to be more clearly defined in the American Federal period that followed after the revolution.

The colors of American Early Georgian, however, were of brighter, lighter, and cleaner tints than in England—and this is one noticeable difference. Although many of the Williamsburg colors are on the medium and deep side, other Georgian homes in Virginia, Charleston, Philadelphia, favored the pastel. Climate may have had something to do with this, for paler colors are generally preferred in sunny regions.

The Classical revival struck America, just as it did France and England. It is doubtful, however, if the great Johann Winckelmann had much of a direct influence. American revolution was responsible for the Federal style and, at the beginning of the nineteenth century, an Empire taste.

The flourishing of Robert Adam in England was during a time when America was far from friendly, hence not much Adam furniture was brought here or made here. Hepplewhite and

THE WOODWORK IN THE PARLOR OF PRENTIS HOUSE, NEW ENG-
LAND (ABOUT 1733) IS A RICH MEDIUM GREEN ON THE WARM
SIDE, WITH WHITE ON PLASTER WALLS. COURTESY, SHELBURNE
MUSEUM, INC. PHOTOGRAPH BY EINARS J. MENGIS.

AS TYPICAL OF MANY EARLY AMERICAN HOMES, HERE IN THE
DINING ROOM OF PRENTIS HOUSE WOODWORK WAS STAINED A
RICH TERRA COTTA RED. WALLS WERE WHITEWASHED. COURTESY,
SHELBURNE MUSEUM, INC. PHOTOGRAPH BY EINARS J. MENGIS.

Sheraton, however, who were a trifle later in time, were eagerly accepted.

Thomas Jefferson did much to influence American taste in decoration. It is said that the architecture of Williamsburg filled him with scorn, no doubt because of his political memories. As a scholar and capable architect himself, he would restore the Classical ideal which to him recalled the great republics of Greece and Rome. He designed Monticello and the University of Virginia and, with other designers that followed, reoriented American taste.

For at least fifty years thereafter the beauty of the Georgian era went into decline—only to come back into favor as its magnificence was seen in true perspective. While Jefferson's classicism still exists in large scale in Washington, D.C. and just about every state capitol, its quality was far too formal, intellectual, and strict for dwellings in which to live a normal life. For such purpose Georgian was and is more comfortably designed.

In the patriotism of the Federal style, much was drawn from France. There was friendship with Louis XVI and Napoleon. Both George Washington and Thomas Jefferson brought

French furniture and taste to America along with French colors. Out of them came what is no doubt the most authentic and original of American architectural and interior styles. It entered the White House under Jefferson and was there until the British destroyed it in 1814. (The able restoration of James Monroe, in 1817, brought it closer to French Empire.)

Every region of eastern United States had its Federal examples. There were the magnificent designs of Samuel McIntire in Salem built from the wealth of sea captains and merchants. There were plantation homes in the south with the air of Italian villas. Every eastern state had dwellings which, fortunately, are now being restored and preserved. Eminent, of course, was the Colonial church. In the Federal style the Greek column and pilaster were distinctive marks, together with motifs drawn from eagles, trumpets, thunderbolts, wreaths, etc. The best of furniture was typified in the creative talents of Duncan Phyfe of New York.

As happened with styles in other countries, American Federal later shifted toward Empire and got fussier and more archaeological (as it did in French Directoire and Empire and in

HERE IN THIS ROOM FROM H. CLAY BROWN HOUSE, CHESTER-
TOWN, MARYLAND (1762) IS THE GEORGIAN STYLE AT ITS SIMPLE
AND ELEGANT BEST. WALLS ARE A PALE, WARM GREEN. PHOTO-
GRAPH COURTESY HENRY FRANCIS DU PONT WINTERTHUR MU-
SEUM.

THE HARVEST ROOM OF DUTTON HOUSE, NEW ENGLAND (ABOUT
1782) WOULD BE IN THE HOME OF A PROSPEROUS BUT NOT ARISTO-
CRATIC FAMILY. THE WOODWORK IS A VIVID TURQUOISE GREEN,
THE WALLS WHITE WITH STENCILLED DESIGNS. COURTESY SHEL-
BURNE MUSEUM, INC. PHOTOGRAPH BY EINARS J. MENGIS.

THIS POST-REVOLUTIONARY ROOM IS IN THE ROBERT MOORE HOUSE, PETERSBURG, VIRGINIA (CA. 1800) AND SHOWS ADAM INFLUENCES. THE WALLS ARE GOLD SILK WITH WHITE WOODWORK AND TRIM. PHOTOGRAPH COURTESY THE METROPOLITAN MUSEUM OF ART.

THIS ROOM, DESIGNED BY SAMUEL McINTIRE, FAMOUS AMERICAN ARCHITECT AND CRAFTSMAN, IS IN THE FEDERAL STYLE OF THE EARLY NINETEENTH CENTURY AND DEFINITELY CLASSICAL. WALLS ARE A SOFT YELLOW-GREEN. DRAPERIES AND UPHOLSTERY ARE GOLD. PHOTOGRAPH COURTESY HENRY FRANCIS DU PONT WINTERTHUR MUSEUM.

English Regency). The colors also went from pastels to deeper tones. Then, after 1850, came the Romantic Era which led to Victorianism.

There is much about American taste in color that is unique and original, and which complements both the nature of the countryside and the character of the people. The frugal style of Early Colonial is provincial and will be touched upon in the next chapter. Not much color was used beyond white, iron oxide red, ochers, and some green. These hand-wrought homes held few luxuries and, of course, virtually no pretensions.

The Early Georgian style, typified at Williamsburg, is directly British, and most of the furnishings came from England. Thus Chart 7, English through Early Georgian, is quite authentic for America as well. Anyone wishing to feature pre-revolutionary taste, with a background of wealth may refer to it.

Chart 8, English Late Georgian and after, does not reflect American preference as well as Chart 7. There is a pertinent reason for this. With the revolution, America cut ties with England as well as gained its own mind and individuality. As has been mentioned, the Adam style of the late eighteenth century did not make a great deal of progress here. In its place came American Federal which contained as many French elements as English, but was

essentially American in quality and the native conception of American architects, interior designers, and furniture manufacturers—not to forget silversmiths, glass blowers, and artisans in all home crafts.

It would be good tradition, therefore, to accept the colors of Chart 7 as authentic for America up to the time of revolution. Those on Chart 8, however, are less significant. The reference, for American, can thus shift from Chart 7 to Chart 9 (page 103).

Incidentally, the French colors of Charts 5 and 6 should not be neglected. These styles flourished under conditions of wealth, royalty, and sophistication which stand in marked contrast with the early and more democratic American way of life. None the less, they would apply if the French "touch" is desired. French Empire, however, definitely influenced America because of the close friendship of the two nations. The Empire manner was featured in the White House and has been restored only recently.

Chart 9, devoted to American Period Styles, shows an excellent cross-section of colors featured in American homes during Colonial and Federal times up to the beginning of the nineteenth century. (English Early Georgian colors, as on Chart 7, should be included.)

To discuss them in their order of appearance on the chart, Salem White was widely applied, particularly for upper walls. Americans used more white than did the English or French, probably because they applied fewer wall coverings.

Newport Yellow and Virginia Green are quite American. Tones of pale yellow-green, in fact, are quite individual to the taste of this nation. The same is true of gold variations, such as Windsor Gold, Charleston Green, Perry Gold. These are typically American and were usually applied to woodwork, often with white above.

There was also generous use of gray, such as Dove Gray and Vernon Gray, both for woodwork and walls. Chart 9 includes Colonial Green which is cooler and brighter than the English Georgian Greens of Chart 7.

Cupboard Red is very American. It was used to line cabinets as well as to coat woodwork. Regardless of wall color, the corner cabinet usually revealed Cupboard Red.

THE WEST PARLOR AT MOUNT VERNON HAS WALLS OF A SOFT, WARM GRAY. PHOTOGRAPH COURTESY THE MOUNT VERNON LADIES' ASSOCIATION.

THIS IS THE BANQUET HALL AT MOUNT VERNON. THE STYLE IS CLASSICAL. WALLS ARE A COOL BLUE-GREEN, WITH TRIM AND WAINSCOT IN BUFF. PHOTOGRAPH COURTESY THE MOUNT VERNON LADIES' ASSOCIATION.

A few of the colors of Chart 9 are taken from Mount Vernon, which is Late Georgian. Vernon Gray is found in the west parlor, Vernon Rose on the woodwork of the east parlor. Vernon Blue is in the banquet hall. Washington Gold, a soft and refined tone, is the color of the woodwork in Washington's bedroom where he died on December 14, 1799. The upper walls are off-white.

At the bottom of Chart 9 are three colors from the White House at Washington, D.C. These are definitely Empire and date to the early nineteenth century: the Red Room, the Blue Room and the Green Room. The wall treatment is silk damask. While the Green Room chip on Chart 9 is a close match, the original for the Red Room is purer and stronger. The Blue Room chip would, to be precise, require slightly more purity.

The influence here is French and evokes the era of President Monroe. Thankfully, these White House rooms—as well as others—have lately been restored to their original and stately beauty after several generations during which Victorian fancies threw them out of character.

9 PROVINCIAL AND NATIVE TASTE

Every nation has its provincial style. The term is loosely used to distinguish the informal mode of life from the formal, the town or hamlet from the big city, the countryside from the court, the man of substance and quality from the hereditary aristocrat. The provincial style may embrace anything from a costly mansion to a simple hut. It is provincial because it is *away* from fashion and convention. It is architecture, furniture, and decoration meant for living and not mere show. It derives from that which is practical, comfortable, friendly, and honest. It is nearly aways a *mixture* of periods and styles. While it is born of imitation in some respects, it is fundamentally an expression of people whose taste is guided by matters of utility, frugality, and economy. There may be planned extravagance in the pure period style. In the provincial style, people put together what they have, waste nothing, and create beauty from things at hand.

To carry out the sequence that has been followed in this book—from French to English to American — the provincial style of the French will be touched upon first. The French home was well constructed. Because of the scarcity of wood, there was considerable masonry, such as red tile roofs. Inside, there were exposed oak beams and columns, with rough plaster for walls. The floor was red tile like the roof, but in a honeycomb pattern.

During the latter days of Louis XV and XVI, many noblemen left the courts and many rich bourgeoisie left Paris to settle in the provinces. Many were fairly well off financially. They were educated and intelligent, and they brought with them knowledge and memory of French achievements in the fine and domestic arts. There was a certain spirit of revolt in this back-to-the-land movement. If the luxuries of aristocracy and wealth were to be emulated—which they were—they must also be stripped down and given practical interpretations.

French Provincial has recently seen a revival in America. The style of furniture is quite beautiful, for it echoes Louis XIV, XV, and XVI and yet lacks refined (and degenerate) pretensions. The lines and proportions are exquisite. The wood, however, may not be lacquered or varnished but merely waxed or oiled to resist abuse. In upholstery, ornate brocades give way to mere stripes, checks, or textures. Many cabinets, beds, bookcases, are built in. Any carving or gilding is restrained. There are uses for brick and wrought iron—a sort of rustic feeling, as Voltaire might express it, of wooden shoes going up the stairs while silken slippers are coming down.

Above all, there is a mixture of design and no true adherence to period. The rooms are of medium size, well proportioned, graceful, and

AN ATTRACTIVE EXAMPLE OF FRENCH PROVINCIAL DECORATION, THIS ROOM DISPLAYS A COMBINATION OF RUSTIC AND SOPHISTICATED TASTE AT ONE AND THE SAME TIME. IT IS A LITTLE OF ANY AND ALL FRENCH PERIODS. PHOTOGRAPH COURTESY JACQUES BODART, INC.

mellow. In color, and to French preference, typical hues would be Cloud White, Powder Pink, or Pompadour Blue as on Chart 5, or French Rose or Azure Blue as on Chart 6. All can be accepted as authentic French Provincial colors. Wallpaper of a French or Chinese quality, would also be indigenous.

Across the Channel, in Great Britain, the provincial manner was quite different. Here it arose from a medieval background and from the "hustlement" of the great hall, where everything went on more or less at once, to the stout and secure cottage.

Progress was slower in England. The baron or aristocrat was less sophisticated. Thus the English Provincial style was cruder and simpler, well typified in the Elizabethan cottage and Jacobean and Queen Anne details. Also much of the Georgian feeling developed into provincial building and decoration.

The English smaller home was built around the hearth. When men no longer had to live in fear behind moats and stone walls, climate still forced them to seek shelter and security. The hearth, the "ingle nook," was at the center. Here bacon could be cured, clothes dried, food cooked and eaten, and bodies kept warm. Comfort naturally followed. There were rungs on the front legs of chairs to keep the feet off the ground. Chests were for sitting as well as storing. There were chairs, tables, beds that opened out to conserve space—and some that could be taken apart easily for transportation. Even today and even in the numberless "flats" of London and the big cities, central heating is rare. The Englishman needs his hearth and

THIS BEDROOM OF A FRENCH NORMANDY HOME OF THE LATE EIGHTEENTH CENTURY SHOWS THE SIMPLIFICATION OF COURTLY FRENCH STYLES IN A PROVINCIAL SETTING. WOODWORK IS WHITE. NOTE TILE FLOOR WHICH IS RED. PHOTOGRAPH COURTESY THORNE EUROPEAN ROOMS IN MINIATURE, THE ART INSTITUTE OF CHICAGO.

HERE IS A COMBINATION KITCHEN AND DINING ROOM IN AN ENGLISH COTTAGE INTERIOR OF THE EIGHTEENTH CENTURY. CONSTRUCTION IS HALF-TIMBER WITH PLASTER-FILLED WHITE WALLS. FLOOR IS NATURAL FLAGSTONE. FURNITURE AND INTERIOR DESIGN OF THIS PRACTICAL ORDER WERE RECALLED BY THE EARLY SETTLERS OF NEW ENGLAND. PHOTOGRAPH COURTESY THORNE EUROPEAN ROOMS IN MINIATURE, THE ART INSTITUTE OF CHICAGO.

THE THOMAS HART HOUSE IN IPSWICH, MASSACHUSETTS (1640) IS A HALF-TIMBER HOME REMINISCENT OF THE ENGLISH TUDOR-ELIZABETHAN COTTAGE. WHILE GOOD TASTE IS EXPRESSED, PRACTICABILITY IS PARAMOUNT. PHOTOGRAPH COURTESY HENRY FRANCIS DU PONT WINTERTHUR MUSEUM.

THE KITCHEN OF THE MILLBACH HOUSE WHICH WAS PENNSYL-VANIA DUTCH, LIKE THE REST OF THE HOMES OF THIS DILIGENT PEOPLE, HAD A PROSPEROUS AIR ABOUT IT. IN THE ROOM, EVERY-THING IN SIGHT—FURNITURE, POTTERY, TEXTILES, UTENSILS—WAS HAND MADE. COURTESY, PHILADELPHIA MUSEUM OF ART, PHOTO-GRAPH BY A. J. WYATT, STAFF PHOTOGRAPHER.

much of his home life is designed around it.

As in France, beams were exposed and filled between with plaster. Much color was used. Edwin Foley writes that the provincial Englishman delighted in color. There are few records of this taste, however, for things humble have faded and been lost to history. Yet from what is known of Stuart, Queen Anne, and Early Georgian, it would be fairly safe to conclude that ivory and green were popular. Examples will be found on Chart 7: Tudor Buff, Stuart Ivory, Queen Anne Green, Light Georgian Green. These probably would be authentic.

A remarkably good definition of the provincial or native style was written by Francis Bacon: "Houses are made to live in, and not to looke on. Therefore let Use bee preferred before Uniformitie." In France there had been much that was meaningless in the way of needless frills and adornments. Some of this was stripped away in the French Provincial style, and even more in the English Provincial.

But it took America really to get down to earth. Here living conditions were completely different from those of Britain or Europe. There were no medieval castles and communities, no invading armies and prolonged wars, no royal palaces or cathedrals, no museums or classical ruins to dig up and emulate. True, wood blockhouses and barricades were needed on occasion to protect against the Indian, but it didn't take long before peace was across the land. If there was adversity to face, it came from mother nature, the struggle for food, shelter, and survival.

To a large extent Early Colonial was provincial in its hand-wrought and practical beauty. As in English Provincial, furniture was primarily for use, not appearance. The Colonial craftsman soon demonstrated an individuality and originality of his own. Native arts took on a character suited to the new land.

The Shakers, for example, who settled in northern New York and New England, made free use of different woods. For religious reasons, perhaps, their ideas of design and decoration were simple and uncomplicated. However, while the Shakers used little color, the German settlers of Pennsylvania delighted in it. Here the free use of color, of charming patterns of fruits, flowers, animals, birds, and people so well known to Americans today established a truly provincial style. Itinerant artists, joiners, and cabinetmakers developed local styles over the land, many of them independent of British origin. Having considerable native skill, they would go from town to town or home to home, building cabinets and furniture or painting and stenciling walls from quaint patterns.

There were also the local cabinetmakers whose creations bring fantastic prices today at auctions and who developed styles and motifs which became distinguished marks in trade.

American Provincial is rustic on one hand and refined on the other. In the humbler arts and crafts there are hooked rugs, crocheted or patchwork quilts, needlepoint, painted tole trays, stenciled furniture, cabinet and wall designs, spattered floors. Here the look is casual, and the style is frank and direct.

In upper class provincial, there is a charming blend and mixture which is taste at its demo-

WHILE MANY OBJECTS AND SURFACES OF PENNSYLVANIA DUTCH FURNITURE AND DECORATION WERE LEFT UNPAINTED, THERE WAS A FREE USE OF COLOR AND DECORATION ON CABINETS, WALLS AND WOODWORK—PLUS BRIGHTLY HUED CRAFTS OF EVERY VARIETY. PHOTOGRAPH COURTESY OF THE METROPOLITAN MUSEUM OF ART.

THE LIVING ROOM OF A SHAKER COMMUNITY HOUSE (CA. 1800)
REFLECTS THE AUSTERITY OF THIS RELIGIOUS GROUP. IN THE DEC-
ORATIVE ARTS, THEY CREATED GREAT BEAUTY, WHOLLY LACKING
IN PRETENSE, AND BUILT UPON ECONOMY, DIRECTNESS, AND HON-
ESTY OF CRAFTSMANSHIP. WOODWORK WAS OFTEN BLUE, WITH
PAINTED FURNITURE IN DULL RED, MUSTARD YELLOW, AND GREEN.
PHOTOGRAPH COURTESY THORNE AMERICAN ROOMS IN MINIA-
TURE, THE ART INSTITUTE OF CHICAGO.

THE NEW ENGLAND COLONIAL BEDROOM, AS TYPIFIED HERE, WAS
POPULAR FOR WELL OVER A HUNDRED YEARS FROM 1750 ON—AND
ITS CHARM IS STILL REPEATED AND REVERED. WALL DECORATIONS
IN THIS CASE WERE STENCILLED OVER WOOD OR PLASTER IN
SIMPLE HUES. PHOTOGRAPH COURTESY THORNE AMERICAN ROOMS
IN MINIATURE, THE ART INSTITUTE OF CHICAGO.

cratic best. Many American homes of the eighteenth and early nineteenth centuries combine Early Colonial with importations and reproductions from England, France, Holland, China — indeed, from practically all parts of the civilized world.

If one goes beyond the Alleghenies, there is the Natchez and New Orleans home, the great mansions of Tennessee and Kentucky—to the mid-west, southwest, far west, true American provinces. And everywhere, throughout the country, there is further individuality.

America, of course, is a land of many peoples, races, and nationalities. Its style is a cross-section of different tastes. Yet somehow there is an American style, actually a harmonious composite of the styles of many cultures.

As to color, there is no strict palette, such as to be seen at Williamsburg or in the Late Georgian and Federal styles. Probably any of the colors on Chart 9 would be authentic—and many also from Charts 7 and 8 devoted to England, and Charts 5 and 6 devoted to France.

THE BEGINNINGS OF THE VICTORIAN STYLE AROUND 1840 WERE QUITE ELEGANT—BEFORE CHAOS SET IN. THE DRAWING ROOM SHOWN HERE IS COMPOSITE. THE WALLS ARE GREEN, THE DRAPERIES AND CARPET BRIGHT RED. PHOTOGRAPH COURTESY THORNE EUROPEAN ROOMS IN MINIATURE, THE ART INSTITUTE OF CHICAGO.

10 THE DECADES OF VICTORIANISM

Few people these days are interested in the Victorian era as a period in the history of decoration. As a matter of fact, Victorianism was more of a way of life, and a mighty ludicrous and fanciful one. It gave the world sentimentalism in music and art, pseudo-morality in thought, saccharine romance in literature and, along with them, a fantastic array of architectural curiosities. If it marked a low ebb in the art of design, its expression was unique and worthy of a special chapter and color chart.

Victoria was the granddaughter of George III and the niece of the dissipated George IV. Her reign lasted for sixty-four years, from 1837 to 1901. She was queen at eighteen, married her beloved Albert at twenty-one, gave birth to nine children, and became a much bereaved widow at forty-two, living forty years thereafter and dying at the age of eighty-two.

Though Albert was never too popular with the British public, his marriage to Victoria was an idyllic one. He was a wise man, tall, handsome, cultured, and liberal. If the period in which he lived is justly called the Victorian,

Albert as Prince Consort was certainly its leading spirit. Elected president of the Society of Arts in 1847, he sponsored a series of exhibits designed to arouse interest in "art manufacturers" which led in 1851 to the Great Exhibit of the Crystal Palace. This exhibit, one of gigantic proportions and influence, spread Victorianism everywhere and was emulated two years later in New York.

The age was "distinguished" by an endless reach for novelty and for pretensions in design which many persons today still recall. It was supported by machine processes, lathes and

jig-saws, which replaced the craftsmen and led to the most ornate, fussy, and ridiculous fripperies known to history.

If there is a Victorian style, it is any and all things at one and the same time. It is unique because of its conglomeration. Originally begun as a Gothic revival, it went into things Egyptian, Turkish, Moorish, Greek, Byzantine, Persian, Venetian, Chinese, French Baroque and Rococo. It took ludicrous pride in obelisks, minarets, towers, gables, parapets; in tents, fountains, porches, verandas, pagodas, pavilions; in cast iron fences, vases, deers, and Newfoundland dogs; and it still scars numberless cemeteries with grotesque headstones, monuments, and tombs.

Much of Victorian interior decoration reflects the secluded and sheltered position of women. The Queen herself was retiring. For the Centennial at Philadelphia in 1876 she sent, as her contribution and from her own hand, a group of etchings and two linen napkins. In the Victorian home sat the woman who was "only a bird in a gilded cage." She cultivated the arts with a vengeance, took drawing lessons, music, dancing, and French and busied herself with a fantastic assortment of august trivialities. And when not at home, she spent her time, properly escorted, attending bazaars where she burdened herself with further gewgaws.

As to the decorative arts of the Victorian Era, some of the furniture was quite attractive and is being reproduced these days. There were chairs and davenports, ottomans, stools, sideboards, tables, beds made of dark mahogany, black walnut, oak, rosewood—not to forget bamboo, the horns of cattle, and wrought iron.

These were days of gaslight, a formal and an informal parlor, bay windows, Godey's Lady's Book, Kate Greenaway children, lithographic printing, ornate printing types. Scroll saw decorations, papiermâché ornaments, stag heads, stuffed birds, flowers under glass, all were in profusion. In the details of the home were beadwork, heavy draperies with tassels and fringe, painted china, embroidered mottoes, needlepoint, decalcomanias, Berlin work and samplers made from printed designs, cut glass and leaded glass, busts, pedestals, Cashmere and Paisley shawls, gift books and albums, Japanese fans, sea shells, lambrequins, and antimacassars.

Because Albert liked to hunt in Scotland, there was a rage for plaids. Encaustic tile was everywhere and knick-knacks were in profusion. Carpets displayed bold patterns in naturalistic motifs and colors. Woodwork came in many deep and lurid finishes. Wallpaper covered walls and ceilings and featured large designs in candent hues. There was much use of marble and of surfaces painted and grained to imitate marble, wood, stone.

Practically everything had a revival and became a fancy during these sixty-four years. Albert was forever busy with the promotion of his "art manufacturers." Sir Walter Scott had erected a baronial castle at Abbotsford and had started many vogues and fads, mostly medieval in flavor to complement his novels. He had gloried in deep red.

Scott's advent had been early, around 1824, and a grand spree had followed which had led England, with America, into the weirdly entangled bowels of Victorian indulgence.

Then in 1861 a reaction took place, sparked by the pre-Raphaelite artists, notably John Ruskin and William Morris. There was a bitter attack on the low state of English taste. Morris sought revolt against the machine and the restoration of fine craftsmanship. He and his associates designed furniture and set up shop as decorators. There would be no further sham. The art of interior design, divorced from life, would be re-wed to it. Whistler also took a hand, and his famous Victorian Peacock Room may be seen today at the Freer Museum in Washington, D.C.

Also important to the attempted reform was Charles Lock Eastlake, an accomplished scholar in the arts (and translator of Goethe's *Theory of Color*). If Eastlake did not do too well in Great Britain, a book of his with the modest title, *Hints on Household Taste*, created a furor in America. Every home had to own a copy. It endeavored to set new values and it illustrated whereof it spoke. Eastlake

THERE IS HARDLY A SQUARE INCH NOT ADORNED WITH DESIGN,
COLOR, OR GILT IN THE DRESSING ROOM OF JOHN D. ROCKEFELLER
HOME. YET FOR ALL ITS JUMBLE, THE EFFECT HAS CONSIDERABLE
CHARM. PHOTOGRAPH BY GOTTSCHO-SCHLEISNER.

abjured superfluities, gaudy wallpaper, useless ornaments. Although his heart was in the right place, the popularity of his views got out of hand. Furniture and decoration in the Eastlake manner violated and misinterpreted the man and became an unfortunate epithet.

Morris, Eastlake, and their confreres had little success and what they created is virtually unknown today. It is even doubtful if their taste was good by modern standards. While the design was fair, it was still fussy and too close to the Victorian. The biggest mistake made, perhaps, had to do with color. Morris objected to the brilliant hues of the day and sought to pull them down into subdued "terti-aries." There would be no more pure red, fuchsia, purple, or green but muted and dull variations of rust, ocher, olive, and sage green. Although Morris later repudiated his dull col-

ors and went back to purity, the damage had been done. As is shown on Chart 10 (page 105), the color story of the Victorian era ends on these forlorn notes, for they caught on and became the fashion in the early years of the twentieth century.

In Victorianism, the "Gay Nineties" are known as the Mauve Decade. The color honors William Henry Perkin, who at the age of eighteen discovered the first of the coal-tar or aniline dyes (1856). In various shades of fuchsia, magenta, purple, violet, it was adopted by Victorians and became the symbolic hue of the times. Two historic and authentic examples (Perkins Violet and Victorian Mauve) are shown on Chart 10.

Victorian colors (Chart 10)—in paints, flock wallpaper, and textiles were by and large dark and pronounced. Stuart Green (Hunting Green, Brunswick Green) is typical, although there was far more popularity for Dark Olive. Rich, deep, yellowish greens rank next to mauve and purple as typically Victorian.

Third in tradition would be Pompeii Red (also shown on Chart 4) and Wine Red. It may well be that bright red cut through the false modesty of the Victorian and revealed his true color. Certainly it is odd to associate the most outward and mundane of all hues with the affectation and hypocrisy of the era. No red could possibly be too brilliant for the Victorian, and he gloried in it more as sinner than saint.

Victorian Rose is vanity in imitation of the French. Devon Cream, which lasted through the Victorian period and beyond, was widely used. It betrays the fact that underneath all the histrionic postures of the day, the Victorian's

WHEN VICTORIANISM "LET GO" NEAR THE END OF THE NINE-TEENTH CENTURY, IT WAS INCREDIBLY UGLY AND HAD LOST ALL SENSE OF HARMONY, REASON, OR BALANCE. HERE IS A LIVING ROOM OF 1894. PHOTOGRAPH COURTESY MUSEUM OF THE CITY OF NEW YORK, THE BYRON COLLECTION. PHOTOGRAPH BY BYRON.

soul was as drab as cream or buff. This characterless tint which not too long ago in America outsold all other colors in paint, still haunts Great Britain. It is the survival of the Puritan conscience after an orgy with the spectrum.

Chinese Blue represents better taste. Blue, however, is none too Victorian in spirit. More typical are Tobacco Brown and Taupe which had stuffy and dusty qualities to go along with draperies that drooped and lay over the floor, furniture that was overstuffed, and "Turkish corners" piled high with faded cushions.

Victorianism died of old age and senility shortly after the death of the Queen in 1901. At the time of its slow demise, the popular vogue in furnishings was for Sage Green, Cedar Rust, and Gray Mauve (see Chart 10).

In the immediate wake of Victorianism came a period known as Art Nouveau, to be described at the beginning of the next chapter. To carry on, after World War I, in the Roaring Twenties decoration was monotonous and drab. If the home lost some of its gingerbread, inside and out, decorative replacements were not much of an improvement. Furniture was solid oak or mahogany and took real muscle to lift. Or if wood frames were not in evidence, the upholstery was a foot or so thick, and from it often wriggled coiled steel springs.

After World War I, in the Roaring Twenties, American taste continued to betray indifference. (No one stayed home anyhow.) Wall paints in ivory, cream, and buff smothered everything. Wallpaper, with big patterns and brilliant hues, still flourished. In upholstery fabrics and carpets the leading colors were Burgundy, Dusty Rose, Royal Blue. This carried on until the dynamic years preceding World War II. Then, for the duration of the war period, colors and color trends were held at a complete standstill.

After World War II, and as the next chapter describes, a democratic renaissance struck the nation. Most of the world entered a new and brilliant era of color, architecture, furniture, and interior design. While old traditions were to be revered, the art of color would scale original and impressive heights.

NEW DEMOCRACY OF THE FIFTIES

At the turn of the twentieth century, there was a considerable revolution in the arts which became known as Art Nouveau. Much of it was inspired by John Ruskin and William Morris both of whom had decried the ugliness and decadence of Victorian excesses. This revolution was particularly effective in printing and the graphic arts, in posters, architecture, furniture, and interior design.

One thinks of the book illustrations of Aubrey Beardsley, the designs of Walter Crane, the posters of Toulouse-Lautrec and Pierre Bonnard—the writings of Oscar Wilde, the music of Claude Debussy. There was a new symbolism for the arts, new attention to high standards of craftsmanship, a feeling for the design forms of Japan and the Near East.

The age was one of excellent taste in decoration and decorative elements. Indeed many painters threw over impressionism and naturalism for a highly decorative approach to art.

In America there were notable contributions to Art Nouveau by the architect, Louis Sullivan, whose beautifully decorated buildings set new precedents and have since been accepted as true works of originality and genius. Louis Tiffany (of the jewelry family) developed iridescent glass. He designed glass windows, glass vases and bowls, and the well-remembered leaded glass light fixtures which were hung over dining tables throughout the nation.

And toward the end of the period, there was the startlingly original prairie homes of Frank Lloyd Wright. In these early years of the twentieth century, Wright designed, not alone the exterior of the house, but its interiors, its cabi-

FURNITURE AND INTERIOR STYLING LIKE THIS, INTRODUCED DURING THE FIFTIES, ESTABLISHED A DEFINITE AMERICAN PERIOD AND DID MUCH TO REVOLUTIONIZE NATIONAL HOME LIFE. THIS IS THE JOHNSON HOUSE IN EASTHAMPTON, LONG ISLAND, BY GEORGE NELSON. FLOOR MATS AND BLINDS WERE NATURAL. ACCENT COLORS IN UPHOLSTERY AND CUSHIONS WERE RED AND BLUE. PHOTOGRAPH BY ALEXANDRE GEORGES.

nets, furniture, lamps, carpets, textiles.

The colors of the Art Nouveau period were inclined to be heavy and remindful of Victorianism. Decorations were carried out in flat tone having bold outlines. Earth types of colors were preferred, soft, grayish, and muted. Such taste would be extended for a number of years, the drabness mentioned at the end of the last chapter prevailing through two world wars. Then there would be a spectacular change.

HOLIDAY HOUSE AT QUOGUE, LONG ISLAND, WAS CREATED BY GEORGE NELSON DURING THE EARLY FIFTIES. COLOR WAS SIMPLY AND BOLDLY USED. WALL PANELS WERE YELLOW AND BLUE; UPHOLSTERY WAS BRIGHT RED. FLOOR WAS NATURAL. NELSON DESIGNED VIRTUALLY EVERYTHING IN SIGHT.

America found itself in the nineteen fifties, and the era was a unique and phenomenal one for reasons to be explained.

Architecture and decoration on this side of the Atlantic had reached magnificent standards in Colonial and early Federal times. While English influences directly, and French influences indirectly, were clearly evident in American cultural expression—particularly among the moneyed and privileged classes—forms of art and beauty that were wholesome and native in origin also flourished.

There is true quality in the New England home, the red brick houses that crowded the streets of Boston and Philadelphia, the Congregational church that set its spire in the open amid maple and elm trees. Many humble dwellings had their clean and functionally styled furniture and utensils, their simple but colorful and bold decoration. One senses a return to the sacred from the profane, a people born to an optimistic but strict discipline of sedulous work, a people on the way up and not on the way down.

But the Colonial spirit did not last, perhaps because of the industrial revolution which seems to have smothered it, bent it out of shape, and smeared it with soot and grime.

American ingenuity led to the house constructed around a wood frame and to the steel girder skyscraper and factory. Here were ways of enclosing space in a big hurry—and never mind how things looked. Soon the cities of the land were filled with plain or glorified shacks, with row upon row of wood cottages fit for blight, apartment houses with face brick on the front and common brick on the sides and back.

And when the Victorian style appeared, it spread like a plague, scarring architecture with frightening and monstrous deformities. Probably no nation on earth had ever accepted and adjusted itself so well to ugliness. (Of all this, the Pueblo Indian with his adobe abodes, remained a serene master.)

There have been beautiful homes and edifices built in America but they have been the

THE ROBBINS HOUSE, TOLEDO, OHIO, WAS DESIGNED AND BUILT DURING THE FIFTIES. CREDIT GEORGE NELSON FOR ARCHITECTURE, FURNITURE, COLOR. BRICK AT REAR WAS A PINKISH BUFF. CEILING WAS NATURAL FIR. SEATING UNIT WAS UPHOLSTERED IN ORANGE. STORAGE DISPLAY UNIT FEATURED WHITE, ORANGE, GREEN. CHIMNEY AND TABLES WERE WHITE.

THIS GUEST ROOM, DESIGNED BY WILLIAM PAHLMANN IN THE EARLY FIFTIES, WAS IN A COUNTRY HOME. WALLS AND WINDOW CURTAINS WERE OFF-WHITE. CARPETING WAS SAGE GREEN. BEDSPREADS WERE BITTERSWEET ORANGE, WITH BOTTOM DUST RUFFLES IN LIME GREEN.

exception rather than the rule. Then at the turn of the century a revolution began. It was slow, and it still is under way. Before and after World War I, millions of structures continued to plod in the old ruts. Many a purist will insist that ugliness still prevails. But if it does, the American attitude has changed radically. Mediocrity is going out of fashion. A high standard of living, a freer and *al fresco* sort of life, has put a well-afforded premium on good appearance and honest utility—as against mere banality or pretense.

In the subject of this book—color and decoration—the author feels that the nineteen-fifties marked a new American period which may well go down in history as distinct and memorable. This is true of conceptions of architecture, furniture, and decoration—and it is most certainly true of color.

In architecture, Gothic Victorianism was attacked by a new generation of functional designers, by influences of the Bauhaus and Scandanavia. The furbelows were stripped away, and materials were used honestly and unaffectedly. In interior design, Charles Eames, George Nelson, Edward Wormley, Florence Knoll, Finn Juhl and others intro-

NOTE THE BLEND OF PERIOD AND MODERN IN THIS LIVING ROOM DESIGNED BY WILLIAM PAHLMANN IN 1951. WALLS WERE BROWN WOOD. CEILING WAS SAGE GREEN. CARPET WAS YELLOW. UPHOLSTERY WAS ORANGE AND BLACK IN SPANISH DESIGN. OTHER COLORS USED WERE BEIGE AND RUSSET.

IN THIS 1954 CONCEPT, THE MOROCCAN SUITE AT THE COLUMBUS HOTEL IN MIAMI, WILLIAM PAHLMANN SHOWED HIS GREAT TALENT FOR HARMONIOUSLY MIXED ELEMENTS. WALLS WERE DARK BROWN WITH WHITE STRIPE. THE CEILING WAS TURQUOISE BLUE. CURTAINS WERE DARK BROWN WITH TASSELS IN ORANGE. RUG WAS IN WHITE, BROWN AND ORANGE. UPHOLSTERY WAS MOSTLY TURQUOISE. PHOTOGRAPH BY RUDI RADA.

WILLIAM PAHLMANN DESIGNED THE TATTOOED LADY BAR AT THE COLUMBUS HOTEL IN MIAMI IN 1955. WALLS WERE CYPRESS. FLOOR HAD A BOLD PATTERN OF GREEN AND BLUE ON BLACK GROUND. WHITE AND BLUE WERE USED FOR ACCENT ON BAR FACE AND BLINDS. THE UPHOLSTERY WAS IN GOLDEN YELLOW, PINK, TURQUOISE BLUE, ORANGE, AND BLACK. PHOTOGRAPH BY RUDI RADA.

duced revolutionary and practical beauty into furniture. Robsjohn-Gibbings, working along classical lines, simplified tradition. William Pahlmann mixed the old with the new and showed Americans a universal style of decoration. There was intelligence and sophistication in all this which, while partly foreign in its inspiration, was quite natural and indigenous to the American way of life.

With it came a like revolution in color. Probably for the first time in all history a massive population was able to express its feelings and heart's desires and not merely pick sparingly from the arbitrary choices of others.

It was in the early fifties that the paint companies of America embarked upon elaborate systems that offered hundreds of color choices in practically every city, town, and hamlet across the land. Where formerly the average citizen had been limited to a dozen or so ready-mixed paint standards (or obliged to resort to special mixing and matching), he now had a world of variety at his command. He could indulge himself in anything he wanted, and out of this freedom came a truly democratic cross-section of American taste.

Refer to Chart 11 (page 107). With an exciting chance to express themselves, here is what Americans preferred in the early years of the nineteen-fifties: Flame Red, Chartreuse, Sulphur Yellow, Pine Green, Avocado, Shell and Pearl Gray—followed very shortly thereafter by Charcoal, Carnation Pink, Bristol Blue.

In the latter part of the decade, Americans switched their fancies to Beige, Nutria, Dry Brown, then tones of Lilac and Sunset Orange. Through all this, tones of Green Gold were high fashion.

What is notable about Chart 11 is that it is very likely the first graphic picture ever drawn that summarizes the wants and desires of millions of persons at a given period. The author is unaware of a similar situation—millions of persons "voting" for hundreds of colors—at any other time in the past.

Chart 11 is highly significant. To begin with, it reveals hidden desires which were radically different from those which the paint industry had assumed: ivory, pale green, peach, soft yellow, light blue. It demonstrated that conservatism and caution in color styling were not wanted. If they existed, it was only because the consumer had been given little choice from which to gratify his feelings.

It is also significant that when millions chose freely from hundreds of colors, they tended to

EDWARD WORMLEY DESIGNED THIS INTERIOR IN THE FIFTIES. THE WALLS WERE NATURAL PANDANUS CLOTH, THE FLOOR TEAK, THE RUG NATURAL, RED, ORANGE, AND BLACK. THE UPHOLSTERED CHAIR WAS BLACK, THE CANE CHAIR SEATS ORANGE, BROWN, AND NATURAL STRIPES. PHOTOGRAPH BY J. ALEX LANGLEY.

HAAS HOUSE, MONTEGO BAY, DESIGNED AND FURNISHED BY KNOLL ASSOCIATES, NEW YORK, USED STYLES AND COLORS WHICH WERE TYPICAL OF THE FIFTIES. CARPET WAS LIGHT GRAY, DRAPERIES YELLOW AND OFF-WHITE, FURNITURE IN GOLD, WITH ACCENT COLORS IN PILLOWS.

GORDON HOUSE, HOUSTON, TEXAS, WAS DESIGNED BY KNOLL ASSOCIATES IN 1956. WALLS WERE OFF-WHITE AND RED BRICK. FLOOR WAS PALE, CREAMY GRAY. THERE WERE VIVID ACCENTS OF YELLOW, RED-ORANGE, BLACK IN DOORS, UPHOLSTERY, PILLOWS. PHOTOGRAPH COURTESY KNOLL ASSOCIATES.

reach similar conclusions. The color problem did not get out of hand in the least. There was an evident national frame of mind and emotion, consistent and somewhat overwhelming. It was as if a host of persons, left free to roam in a forest, assembled by intuition or psychic harmony at the same meeting places.

The colors of the fifties, of course, did not last for very long. No matters of style ever hold indefinitely for the simple reason that it is human to want change and avoid repetition. Color trends are thus natural and spontaneous. (Incidentally, they have no relation to so-called forced obsolescence.)

Chart 11 may therefore be set as a bright landmark in the history of color. It relates, of course, to the Creative tradition—though it may in the future be recorded as a period style. It is creative, however, in terms of millions, and this is quite singular in the long and ancient story of color.

CHART 9 FOR CHAPTER 8

These authentic American colors may be supplemented by those on Chart 7 devoted to Early Georgian. The early American feeling for color was refined and few strong hues were used until the Empire Period of the early nineteenth century. Unique are yellows, soft yellow greens and subtle variations of gold. There is little that is pretentious or showy. American taste at its best reflects a sense of comfort, restraint and livableness.

AMERICAN PERIOD STYLES

SALEM WHITE

NEWPORT YELLOW

VIRGINIA GREEN

WINDSOR GOLD

DOVE GRAY

CHARLESTON GREEN

COLONIAL GREEN

PERRY GOLD

CUPBOARD RED

VERNON GRAY

VERNON ROSE

VERNON BLUE

WASHINGTON GOLD

RED ROOM

BLUE ROOM

GREEN ROOM

CHART 10 FOR CHAPTER 10

All the colors shown here are authentic and are taken from examples still fresh in memory and record. The Mauve Decade, which delighted in purples, owes the title to the discovery of aniline dyes in 1856. Except for some use of buff and cream, Victorian colors are mostly deep, rich and heavy. During the latter part of the era, these full colors degenerated to the dull tones shown at the bottom.

THE VICTORIAN ERA

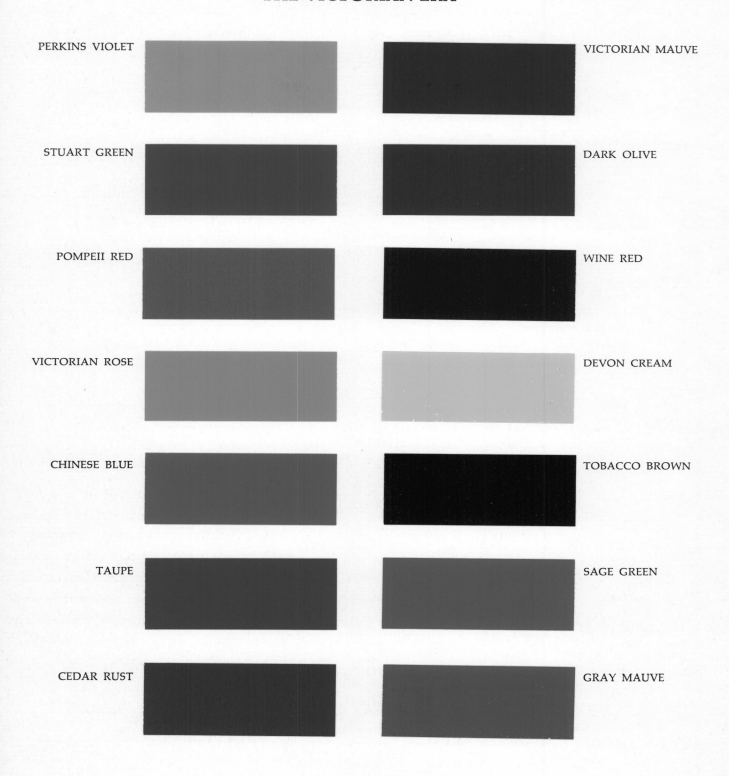

PERKINS VIOLET

STUART GREEN

POMPEII RED

VICTORIAN ROSE

CHINESE BLUE

TAUPE

CEDAR RUST

VICTORIAN MAUVE

DARK OLIVE

WINE RED

DEVON CREAM

TOBACCO BROWN

SAGE GREEN

GRAY MAUVE

CHART 11 FOR CHAPTER 11

In America, the end of World War II brought a revolution in taste. The colors shown here constitute a definite period, complemented by a sudden demand for original modern furniture, decoration and architecture. The samples represent the "free" choice of millions of Americans during the nineteen fifties. The taste is not one of dictation from above but of the democratic insistence of a massive population.

AMERICA: THE FIFTIES

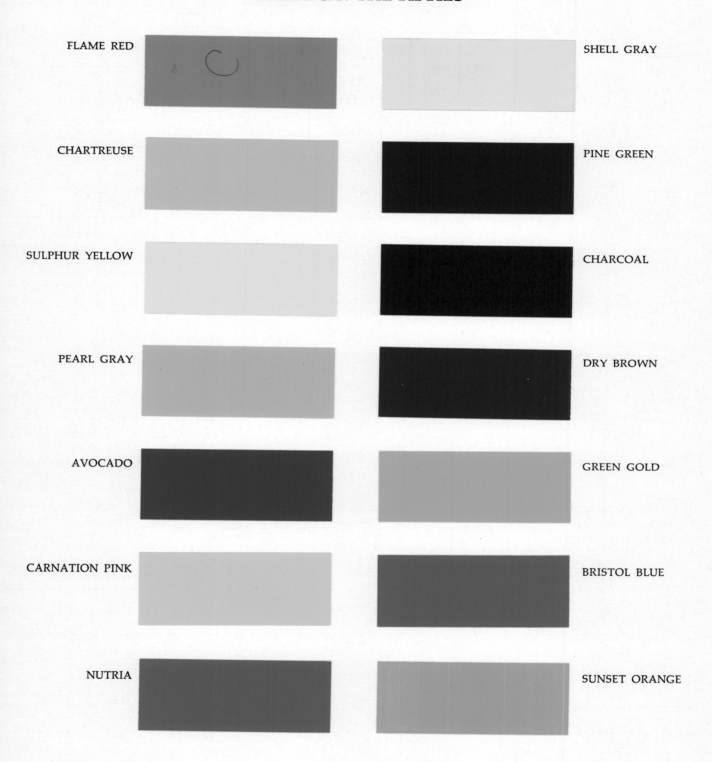

FLAME RED

SHELL GRAY

CHARTREUSE

PINE GREEN

SULPHUR YELLOW

CHARCOAL

PEARL GRAY

DRY BROWN

AVOCADO

GREEN GOLD

CARNATION PINK

BRISTOL BLUE

NUTRIA

SUNSET ORANGE

CHART 12 FOR CHAPTER 5

The colors shown here have been successfully used in the functional decoration of hospitals and schools. Most are soft in tone and carefully adjusted as to brightness. They will appear somewhat cleaner in large area. Because of prolonged occupancy, color effects should be reserved in order to avoid monotony and undue distraction. Of chief importance is the need for reflectances that will reduce glare, hold the eye to a steady adjustment and hence assure comfortable vision.

HOSPITALS AND SCHOOLS

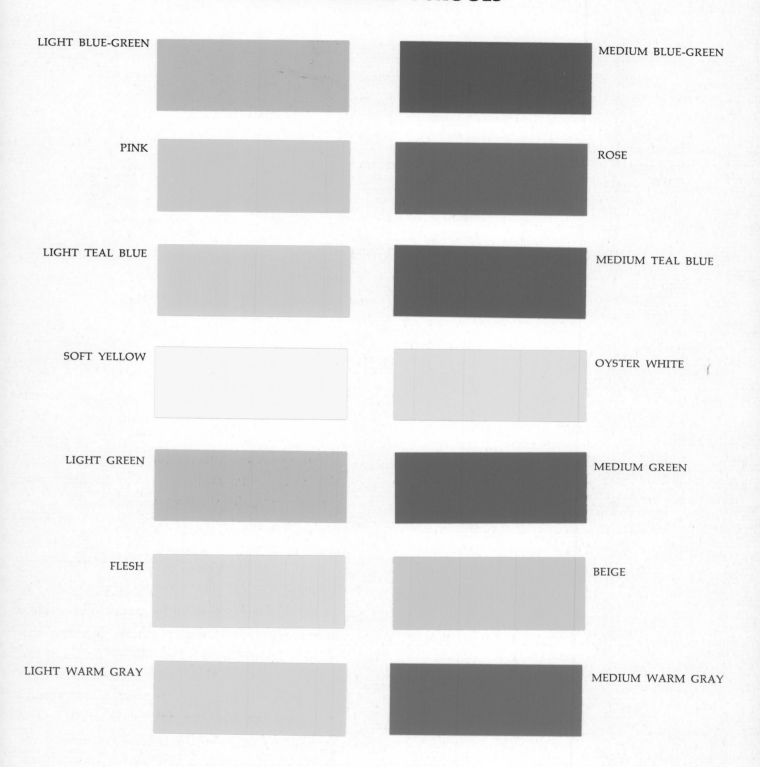

LIGHT BLUE-GREEN

MEDIUM BLUE-GREEN

PINK

ROSE

LIGHT TEAL BLUE

MEDIUM TEAL BLUE

SOFT YELLOW

OYSTER WHITE

LIGHT GREEN

MEDIUM GREEN

FLESH

BEIGE

LIGHT WARM GRAY

MEDIUM WARM GRAY

CHART 13 FOR CHAPTER 16

The importance of color in factories is first to control brightness in the general field of view for an efficient seeing condition. Interiors can then be conditioned for emotional pleasure and interest, using warm, cool, or luminous hues as working conditions suggest. Color should be functional and not merely decorative. The brilliant samples in the second column of the chart are for use as a safety code to mark important hazards.

INDUSTRIAL PLANTS

LIGHT GREEN

MEDIUM GREEN

BEIGE

SANDALWOOD

LIGHT BLUE

MEDIUM BLUE

SOFT YELLOW

SOLAR YELLOW

LIGHT GRAY

ALERT ORANGE

MEDIUM GRAY

FIRE RED

DEEP GRAY

SAFETY GREEN

SPOTLIGHT BUFF

CAUTION BLUE

111

CHART 14 FOR CHAPTER 17

Wider choice of color is appropriate in office buildings. It is well to plan for variety in order to create a desirable change of pace during course of employee traffic. End walls in deeper shades will also lessen monotony and provide useful areas for visual relaxation. As shown on the chart, colors are best when somewhat refined in purity. This will control glare and not distract from visual tasks.

OFFICES

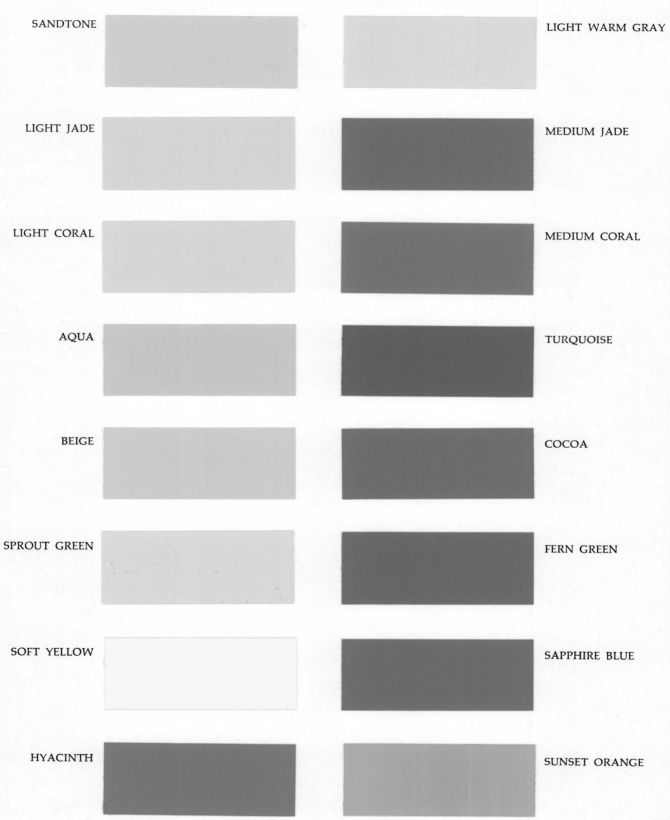

SANDTONE

LIGHT WARM GRAY

LIGHT JADE

MEDIUM JADE

LIGHT CORAL

MEDIUM CORAL

AQUA

TURQUOISE

BEIGE

COCOA

SPROUT GREEN

FERN GREEN

SOFT YELLOW

SAPPHIRE BLUE

HYACINTH

SUNSET ORANGE

CHART 15 FOR CHAPTER 18

In a store, the purpose of color is to attract the eye and create a dynamic and pleasing environment for the sale of merchandise. The colors on this chart have all been researched for average human appeal. They are also relatively bright and clean in tone. Both drabness and extreme high style should be avoided if average emotional responses are to be spontaneous and favorable. There should be variety of color.

STORES

PASTEL PEACOCK

BRIGHT PEACOCK

PASTEL CANARY

BRIGHT CANARY

PASTEL EMERALD

BRIGHT EMERALD

BLOSSOM PINK

FLAME PINK

SKY BLUE

SEA BLUE

PASTEL ORANGE

LIME GREEN

FOREST GREEN

WALNUT BROWN

MAROON

MARINE BLUE

CHART 16 FOR CHAPTER 20

The colors on this chart have been drawn from research on the psychological association existing between colors and foods. All have an "appetizing" quality. They are desirable for use as background or accent in the sale or service of food. While the palette is a restricted one and avoids purples and yellow-greens, it has sufficient variety to allow for many harmonious and dramatic combinations.

FOOD SERVICE

WARM YELLOW

VERMILION

PEACH

MELON

LIGHT SPRING GREEN

MEDIUM SPRING GREEN

BEACH TAN

COFFEE BROWN

LIGHT AQUAMARINE

MEDIUM AQUAMARINE

CANDY PINK

FLAMINGO

WHITE

CASCADE BLUE

PART II MODERN PRINCIPLES

12 THE AGREEABLE ENVIRONMENT

Many architects and interior designers, being thoroughly imbued with the Creative tradition, prefer to look at color intuitively and to evoke matters of taste and talent on a personal basis. While these same men may subscribe to the doctrine of Louis Sullivan that "form follows function," with color they obviously feel that the advice may be disregarded.

Yet color, too, has every need to follow function in many applications. While esthetics and creative originality may be appropriate—and demanded—in a home, an exclusive shop, or a restaurant, they may be out of place in environments where people are expected to do more than sit about and indulge their senses.

In the Classical tradition the ancient respected a type of "functionalism" in his adherence to mysticism and tradition. If he devoted taste to his endeavors, it was in the glorification of that which was prescribed by the customs and civilization of his times. In this he was objective rather than subjective.

There is a new functionalism today that is slowly and steadily coming to influence, if not dominate, the use and application of color. It rises out of an awareness of the fact that there is more to color than superficially greets the eye. While beauty of appearance may be important, it needs control if it is to serve practical ends. Granted that an interior has enough light for clear vision, the color and brightness of the surroundings must be held responsible for the comfortable and efficient conduct of work tasks. The environment is wrong if it needlessly distracts rather than aids vision. It is wrong if it demands undue strain, if it impairs human performance, or otherwise runs contrary to certain obligations expected of it.

In a school, such obligation may be to smooth the course of vision and to relieve emotional tension. In a hospital it may be to serve psychotherapeutic ends, aid visual acuity in the surgery and convalescence in the private room and ward. In a factory it may be to direct attention, mark hazards, build order into what otherwise may be chaos. In an office, it may be to overcome monotony and allow for the efficient performance of difficult visual tasks.

In a store, a hotel, motel, restaurant, theatre, the obligation may be to strike common denominators of public taste that will attract business by appealing to mass psychology—without confusing it or going "over its head." Here the functionalism is present to make money and pay profits.

The chapter that follows will deal with problems of light and illumination and will be concerned with their effective coordination *with* color, not as elements apart from color. For the present, let us refer to recent findings having

THE SCHOOL ENVIRONMENT NEEDS VARIETY, INTEREST, AND
PROPER SCIENTIFIC PRACTICE IN THE CONTROL OF LIGHTING AND
COLOR. PERKINS & WILL, ARCHITECTS. PHOTOGRAPH BY BILL
HEDRICH, HEDRICH-BLESSING.

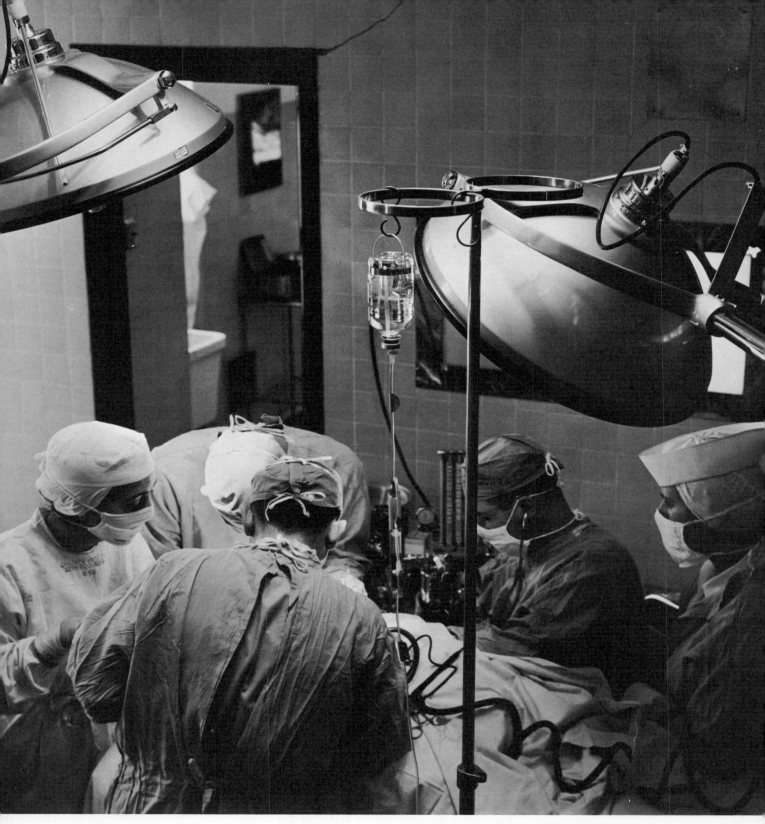

IN HOSPITALS THERE IS NEED FOR SHARP VISUAL ACUITY IN THE SURGERY—AND AGREEABLE COLORS IN PRIVATE ROOMS AND WARDS TO INSPIRE AN ATTITUDE FAVORABLE TO RECOVERY. PHOTOGRAPH BY H. ARMSTRONG ROBERTS.

122

to do with the physiological and psychological effects of color.

The architect and interior designer should please understand that even though color is not subject to academic rules, it most certainly can profit from those principles which are derived from clinical experience.

To begin, it is probably no exaggeration to say that light level is the simplest of all problems to deal with as far as the agreeable environment is concerned. (This, of course, would exclude the technical engineering of a lighting installation.) In effect, a task is set up and light level increased until the job is visible and easily as well as efficiently done. Having accomplished this, however, a number of other qualifying factors arise. The task's surroundings should not be too dark or too bright. Glare and distraction must be eliminated. Some brightness should usually encompass the whole field of view. Shadows should give form and depth to lighted spaces. The total "effect" must be pleasing. The appearance of the worker himself, in his setting, should be acceptable, if not flattering. Thus, beyond light level alone, there must be considerations as to the "quality" of the light, the color tint of the surrounding brightness, the beauty, proportion, and balance of the interior itself. (Not to forget temperature, humidity, noise-level, and all the other elements that make up the indoor "climate.")

The author, who finds himself on the side of the architect and interior designer, is suspicious of pat answers to lighting and color problems. At the same time, however, there is great fascination in the human aspects of an environment.

IN AN OFFICE, GOOD LIGHT AND UNIFORM BRIGHTNESS IN THE FIELD OF VIEW ARE IMPORTANT TO HUMAN EFFICIENCY AND COMFORT. THESE QUALIFICATIONS ARE WELL MET IN THIS INTERIOR. DESIGNS FOR BUSINESS, INC., DESIGNERS. PHOTOGRAPH BY BEN SCHNALL.

IN A FACTORY, THE NEED IS TO KEEP THE WORKER ALERT, TO PREVENT UNDUE VISUAL FATIGUE, AND TO COLOR-CODE HAZARDS. THIS IS A PLANT OF INTERNATIONAL HARVESTER COMPANY, FORT WAYNE, INDIANA. ALBERT KAHN ASSOCIATED ARCHITECTS AND ENGINEERS. PHOTOGRAPH BY TORKEL KORLING, HEDRICH-BLESSING.

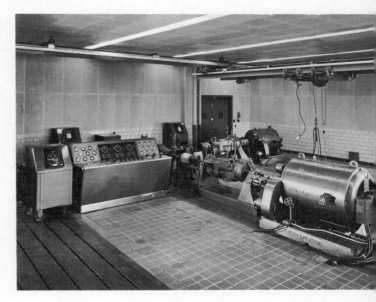

EXCESSIVE CONTRAST IN THE FIELD OF VIEW IS INIMICAL TO GOOD
AND COMFORTABLE SEEING AND SHOULD BE AVOIDED.

WHERE THE FIELD OF VIEW IS VARIED IN COLOR AND BRIGHTNESS,
BUT WITHIN MODERATE LIMITS, VISION IS AT ITS BEST.

SOFTNESS OF COLOR HAS A CENTRIPETAL EFFECT, REMOVES OUT-
SIDE DISTRACTION AND IS CONDUCIVE TO MENTAL CONCEN-
TRATION.

Seeing has to do with many physiological and psychological reactions. To speak in generalities, agreeableness and comfort (like contentment and happiness) are quite relative states, and not very permanent ones at that. They are, in truth, perhaps better expressed in negative than positive terms. Most conceptions of Utopia and green pastures are anything but exciting. Yet where Eden is not-pain, not-strife, not-poverty, not-toil, it becomes a vivid escape.

So, too, for human environments. The good interior is one that is not too dark, not too brilliant, not too hot or cold, or noisy, or dreary, etc. Most people will agree on what they *do not like;* but such universality of view will take any number of directions when it comes to what people *do like!* It would thus seem that there are not, and probably cannot be, definite and incontrovertible specifications for the agreeable environment. Yet such an aim is not hopelessly befuddled. On the contrary, a number of sound, plausible, and fully defensible principles may be intelligently presented. Anyone concerned with human environments would do well to harken to these principles and improve his capacity accordingly.

For example, the human organism is not adapted to unvarying stimuli. (Here is hope and need for variety, the delight of designers.) There is a constant state of flux. All functions rise and ebb continually. Simple thoughts will affect respiration and pulse rate. So pronounced is this tendency for physiological and psychological experiences to fluctuate that they will do so even when the exterior world remains the same. Areas of steady brightness will appear to fade in and out. The pupil opening of the eye will actually close and dilate slightly. Steady sounds will not be heard consistently. Sensations of taste, heat, cold, and pressure will all vary and will be surprisingly independent of unvarying stimuli. If the monotony is long continued, the ability to respond to the stimulus will deteriorate.

People require varying, cycling stimuli to remain sensitive and alert to their environments. Comfort and agreeableness are normally identified with moderate, if not radical, change, and this change concerns brightness and color, as well as all other elements in the environment. If overstimulation may cause distress, so may severe monotony. The prejudice of architects and interior designers against sameness has a sound basis in the facts of life.

Yet if monotony is to be avoided, there is poor reason to kick over the traces and run wild in other directions. In simple terms, where work is performed there is no need to tax the eye for the sake of dramatic effects. If an all-white room appears sterile in the psychological sense, a black-and-white room would be objectionable in the physiological sense.

Both uniformity and excessive contrast are bad. An attempt by the eye to make trying adjustments may well throw it out of kilter. The road to monotony may lead to visual efficiency but to emotional rejection. On the other hand, the road to contrast, though it may lead to emotional acceptance, may impair good visual performance. The place to meet is obviously at the crossroads!

New to the art and science of interior design are recent findings on the physiological effects of brightness and color made under controlled, laboratory conditions. Briefly, the human organism responds in two main directions: in a positive way toward brightness and

IN A STORE, ESTHETIC CONSIDERATIONS CAN SUPPLEMENT GOOD
SCIENTIFIC PRACTICE AS TO ILLUMINATION, BRIGHTNESS, AND
COLOR. VIEW SHOWS GOLDWATERS OF SCOTTSDALE, ARIZONA.
ORIGINAL DESIGN BY PAUL LASZLO. PHOTOGRAPH BY ROBERT
C. CLEVELAND.

warmth of color (red), and in a negative way toward dimness and coolness of color (green, blue). Blood pressure and respiration rate will increase under the influence of red (and brightness) and decrease under the influence of blue (and dimness). In palmar conductance (reaction of the sweat glands which reveals general autonomic arousal), all colors and degrees of illumination will cause effects. This is also true of cortical activation (brain waves). Yet effects will be consistently higher for red than for blue. While no appreciable differences have been noted in changed heart action, frequency of eye-blinks will increase during exposure to red and decrease during exposure to blue.

This means that certain brightness and color effects are possible—*whether or not human beings like them emotionally.* In other words, there is a chance to prescribe brightness and color for definite and functional uses, leaving the element of esthetic appearance more or less open to the taste and personality of the designer. This should please anyone who specifies color, once he grasps the significance of it.

On good evidence it may be said that brightness and color have two major effects. Where the task requires chief attention to the environment, high levels of general illumination and brightness in the surround will condition the human organism accordingly. The attention and interest of the room occupant will be *outward*. This would be a good principle to apply to manual tasks.

On the other hand, where the task requires concentrated visual and mental attention at fixed points (desks and work tables), more subdued brightness in the surround may accomplish the best results. If critical seeing tasks are performed, supplementary localized illumination may be added. In such a setting, attention and interest will be away from the environment and to the job at hand. Man's body and eyes will be physiologically and optically well adjusted.

In purely casual or recreational areas, let it be added, almost anything may be done.

These simple generalities or principles are what have guided the colors selected for the charts of this second section, as well as the specifications suggested for different types of building interiors. Before getting to them, however, there are a few other factors to bring up—illumination and different appearances for color under different degrees of intensity for illumination.

13 ILLUMINATION—QUANTITY AND QUALITY

THE SHIFT OF POPULATION FROM RURAL TO URBAN LIFE BRINGS MILLIONS OF PEOPLE INTO ARTIFICIALLY LIT ENVIRONMENTS. HERE GOOD SCIENTIFIC PRACTICE IN THE CONTROL OF ILLUMINATION IS VITAL TO HUMAN WELFARE.

Lighting is a problem in itself, and one fraught with constant and bitter debate. The author prefers to deal with it in reasonable and human terms and to concentrate on aspects of illumination which relate to appearances for color. In his own experience he has noted major conflict between the lighting specialist (who often argues for high levels) and medical practitioners (who are inclined to plead for moderation). If he takes sides, he tends to favor the ophthalmologist rather than the engineer, for physiological matters seem more important than purely visual or optical ones. After all, the seeing process is a remarkable one. Human vision responds to exceedingly wide limits of intensity—and it sees quite well under very little light.

According to acceptable history in the lighting industry, about 70 years ago Herman Cohn of Germany came to the conclusion that approximately one footcandle was the satisfactory minimum for reading 8-point type in black on white. Over forty years ago in 1917, M. Luckiesh, a prominent American authority, gave three to six footcandles as optimum in libraries. A. P. Trotter, in 1921, specified a required three to four footcandles for library tables. In 1923, J. W. T. Walsh wrote, "For reading and writing, it is now generally agreed that an illumination of about three footcandles is the most comfortable." And in 1924, the so-called Geneva Code of the International Congress on Illumination recommended five footcandles as the minimum quantity of light for school library tables.

Yet by 1941, lighting engineers were claiming that "250 footcandles for reading appears

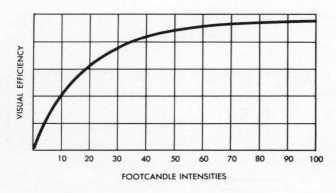

VISUAL EFFICIENCY RISES AS ILLUMINATION INTENSITY IS RAISED
TO A LEVEL OF FROM 30 TO 50 FOOTCANDLES. AFTER THIS, IM-
PROVEMENTS IN SEEING MAY REQUIRE MULTIFOLD INCREASES IN
LIGHT LEVEL.

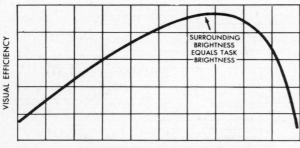

WITH THE BRIGHTNESS OF THE TASK HELD CONSTANT, VISUAL
EFFICIENCY WILL INCREASE AS THE SURROUNDING BRIGHTNESS IS
RAISED TO A LEVEL EQUAL TO OR SLIGHTLY LOWER THAN THE
TASK BRIGHTNESS. HIGHER SURROUNDING BRIGHTNESS MAY LEAD
TO A COLLAPSE IN ACUITY.

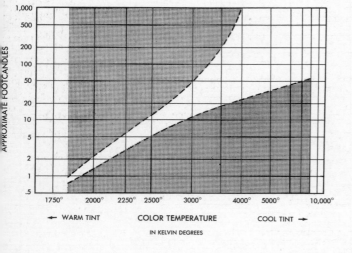

to be below the optimum for easiest reading."
Now this matter has come full circle. Dr. H. R.
Blackwell, in studies sponsored by the Illumi-
nating Engineering Society at the University of
Michigan, reported in 1958 that the illumination necessary to give 8-point type a "supra-
threshold visibility of 15, and to afford a visual
capacity of five assimilations per second with
the maximum accuracy (99%) is, according to
the fount, 1.13 or 1.87 footcandles." So it is
that Blackwell seems to end up where earlier
investigations started.

It is not uncommon for some interiors today
—offices notably—to have several hundred
footcandles. If the eye, according to careful
test, can see fairly well under five footcandles,
how is one to justify the need for a hundred or
more times this much? It is the author's private
view that there really is not much justification.

Although light-level requirements for various tasks have an extensive literature imple-
mented by codes, specifications, and
recommendations, much of this is academic.
Argument here may be specious. The fact that
the eye sees remarkably well over a range from
1 to 1000 (or more) footcandles allows for
wide tolerances. Proponents of high levels may
therefore speak of statistical efficiency, at-
tempting to prove (often correctly) that the
more light, the greater the accuracy.

While a person may hardly object to abundant illumination, there nevertheless are ac-

THIS CHART SHOWS KRUITHOF'S PRINCIPLE AS INTERPRETED BY
THE AUTHOR. THE COLOR TINT OF A LIGHT SOURCE MUST SHIFT
FROM WARM TO COOL WITH INCREASED INTENSITY IF A PLEASANT
OR NATURAL APPEARANCE FOR SURFACE COLOR IN THE FIELD OF
VIEW IS TO BE ASSURED. AT LOW LEVELS, THE MOST "NATURAL"
LIGHT MUST BE ORANGE OR WARM IN TONE. BETWEEN 10-30 FOOT-
CANDLES, YELLOWISH LIGHT (INCANDESCENT) IS SATISFACTORY.
ABOVE 30 FOOTCANDLES WHITE AND BLUISH WHITE TINTS MAY BE
PRESCRIBED.

companying factors to consider. Visibility increases at a rapid rate from darkness to a 50-footcandle level. For added "efficiency" beyond this, light levels may have to be doubled and redoubled. Thus the economics of a lighting installation must be regarded, for while 50 footcandles are fairly easy to achieve, 1500 footcandles, or even 500, may cost quite a bit.

Perhaps the architect or interior designer could settle the matter for himself, and in a wholly practical way. How much would added light cost? Would the expense be offset in cash savings for added efficiency or greater freedom from accidents? Light for the sake of light has small justification. Within reasonable limits, it is very doubtful if the eye itself or the agreeable environment is involved here.

Bear in mind that if there can be too little light, there can also be more than enough. Architects and interior designers (as well as medical people) have objected—and with good cause—to many of the yardsticks set up by lighting authorities in which space-lighting levels are based on visibility for the most difficult tasks that may be performed in them. High-level lighting may be an aid to acuity, but it may also be a handicap if the high light level involves glare or gives great brightness to wall areas. The eye cannot stop itself from looking at, accommodating to, and focusing upon the brightest area in its field of view. Such response is automatic. Therefore, if walls are meaningless in the performance of a visual task, it hardly seems logical to give them the advantage over other elements.

Too, the eye is quick in adjusting itself to brightness and slow in adjusting itself to dimness. If the task is dark (as it might be), and if the surrounding is bright, the whole arrangement from the standpoint of visual efficiency

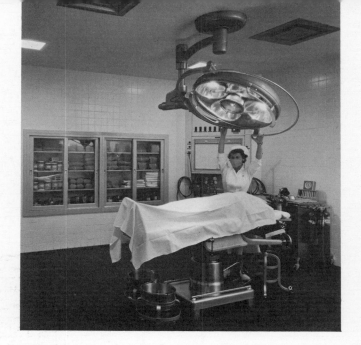

UNDER MANY CONDITIONS, SUCH AS IN THE HOSPITAL SURGERY (THIS ONE IS IN THE MEMORIAL HOSPITAL, BELLEVILLE, ILLINOIS), HIGHLY SPECIAL AND EFFICIENT LIGHT SOURCES ARE DEMANDED. ISADORE AND ZACHARY ROSENFIELD AND HELLMUTH, OBATA & KASSABAUM, INC. ARCHITECTS. PHOTOGRAPH BY ALEXANDRE GEORGES.

GOOD NATURAL AND ARTIFICIAL LIGHT, AND GOOD BRIGHTNESS ENGINEERING, ARE OF MAJOR IMPORTANCE IN SCHOOLS TO PRESERVE AND PROTECT HUMAN EYESIGHT. THIS IS A VIEW OF A ROOM IN THE INDIAN TRAIL SCHOOL IN HIGHLAND PARK, ILLINOIS. PERKINS & WILL, ARCHITECTS-ENGINEERS, CHICAGO, ILLINOIS. PHOTOGRAPH BY SUTER, HEDRICH-BLESSING.

and comfort may be in reverse. Much compensation, incidentally, may be achieved through the use of color.

Thus two points are to be emphasized. First, high light levels (there is an optimum at about 50 footcandles) are rarely necessary—and when they are, extra localized light over specific tasks may be the best answer. Second, with ample illumination provided and assumed, control of the brightness and color of the environment is truly the dominant and most important of all considerations.

While brightness and color contrast will be taken up in the next chapter, let me devote space to an evident but often overlooked phenomenon. Here it is: The element of color tint cannot be divorced from the intensity of a light service if the aim is to achieve appearances that are normal.

The engineering approach often steers clear of color and concentrates primarily on light level and brightness. The reason, of course, is that color is so highly emotional that it becomes a nuisance to consider. Yet, people are likely to place color foremost. Architects well know that, regardless of beauty of form and proportion, some confounded viewer is likely to have complaints about color!

In the light source itself, color is all-important to the truly agreeable environment. No interior, judged esthetically, could possibly be acceptably illuminated with uncorrected mercury or sodium vapor. Their cadaverous effects on human complexion would overwhelm any arguments about visibility or visual efficiency.

In just about every study made on the chromatic quality of light as related to human appearance, warm illumination has been preferred, with ordinary incandescent light rating high. For a pleasant effect, the incandescent lamp and the deluxe, warm-white fluorescent tube would be appropriate. (Tinted bulbs may go too far for general illumination and perhaps even for decorative lamps.)

IN INDUSTRIAL PLANTS, HIGH LEVELS OF LIGHT WILL REDUCE ACCIDENTS BY ASSURING CLEAR VISIBILITY. THIS SAVES HUMAN LIFE, LIMB—AND INSURANCE COSTS. HERE IS A VIEW OF THE NEW DEPARTURE DIVISION PLANT, GENERAL MOTORS CORPORATION, SANDUSKY, OHIO. ALBERT KAHN ASSOCIATED ARCHITECTS AND ENGINEERS. PHOTOGRAPH BY HEDRICH-BLESSING STUDIO.

HERE IS A BEAUTIFULLY ILLUMINATED OFFICE IN THE EQUITABLE ASSURANCE COMPANY, NEW YORK OFFICES. NOTE EVEN DISTRIBUTION OF LIGHT AND YET CLEAR PLASTIC FORM TO ALL OBJECTS. SOFT BRIGHTNESS ON THE WALLS ASSURES IDEAL VISIBILITY. PHOTOGRAPH COURTESY HOLOPHANE COMPANY.

After all, so-called "natural light" is an arbitrary thing. Man knows all sorts of light, from orange-pink dawn and dusk, to yellow sunlight, to white or bluish sky light. He is endowed with a special faculty (known as color constancy) to accept them all as "normal."

A few further notes on the physiological and biological aspects of light and illumination will be given in the chapter on office decoration. For the present, reference is made to an unusual phenomenon which points out the need for the coordination of color tint in light sources with surface colors in an environment in order to achieve natural appearances.

Pertinent here are the findings of A. A. Kruithof of Holland that a pleasing or natural appearance for surface colors (walls, furniture, etc.) will require different tints in a light source, depending on illumination intensity. While this is most important to the agreeable environment, not many architects, interior designers or even lighting engineers are familiar with the phenomenon.

Kruithof writes, "In the first place at a given level of illumination, it is found that the color temperature must lie within certain limits if the effect of the illumination is to be pleasing. Roughly, it may be said that a low or a high color temperature corresponds to a low or high level of illumination, respectively."

The term temperature refers to color and is expressed in Kelvin (K) degrees. It is what the eye sees when a "black body" (such as iron) is heated to incandescence and gives off light. At low temperature, the color tint will be red. It proceeds from here into orange, yellow, white, blue as temperature is increased. Keep the following color temperatures of familiar light qualities in mind in referring to the separate black and white chart devoted to Kruit-hof's principle.

The pinkish and orange tint of twilight varies from about 1750°K to 2500°K.

The common incandescent filament lamp has a temperature of about 2800°K.

Sunlight is about 5000°K.

An overcast sky is about 6000°K.

Blue sky is about 7000°K.

Kruithof states, "For every color temperature there exists a highest and a lowest level of illumination at which the illumination is considered 'pleasing'."

Now give careful study to the chart which illustrates Kruithof's principle. The area of natural or pleasing appearance for surface colors lies in the unshaded space between the two lines.

In brief, beginning with dim light of low intensity, such as might be seen at dawn, surface colors to appear natural require a tinted orange illumination (about 2000°K).

With incandescent light (2800°K) footcandle levels around 10-30 would be optimum. If brighter intensities are used in general room illumination, things may look distinctly yellowish.

With sunlight or the equivalent (5000°K) any level above 30 footcandles would be satisfactory, as indicated on the chart. Any level below 30 would appear "unreal."

Overcast sky daylight or the equivalent (6000°K) requires a minimum of about 40 footcandles—and again the intensity can go higher. If it goes lower than 40, the effect may seem "grayish."

Blue sky daylight or the equivalent (7000°K) requires a minimum of 50 footcandles and can go higher.

THIS WOULD BE CONVENIENCE AND DECORATIVE LIGHTING, ADDING CHARM TO A ROOM LIKE THE GLOW OF A FIREPLACE. YET IT WOULD NOT DO FOR A FULL DAY'S WORK. PHOTOGRAPH BY ALEXANDRE GEORGES.

Looking at things in reverse, whitish or bluish light, if low in intensity (below 30 or so footcandles) will give the world a grayish sort of pallor, an effect that is particularly noticeable at low intensities around or below 5 footcandles. In other words, incandescent light looks natural at *low* levels and strongly tinted at *high* levels. White or bluish light looks natural at *high* levels and unnatural and "ghastly" at low levels.

Fluorescent light sources are frequently identified with Kelvin degrees (3500°, 4500°, etc.). Despite this, however, the illumination they produce may be lacking in red. Hence, "natural" light may not be wholly attributed to them. Kruithof, incidentally, considers a color temperature of about 5500° quite satisfactory for light levels around 100 footcandles. This temperature is equivalent to the so-called de luxe cool white tube which very desirably has red phosphorus and emits a fairly balanced spectrum.

THOUGH NATURAL DAYLIGHT CANNOT BE CONTROLLED, IT IS FREE, TEMPERAMENTAL, AND MAN LOVES TO SEE ITS MANIFESTATIONS. HERE A BROAD SKYLIGHT ON A STAIRWAY WILL TELL THE PERSON INSIDE WHAT GOES ON OUTSIDE—AND SAVE ON THE LIGHT BILL. DESIGNS FOR BUSINESS, INC., DESIGNERS. PHOTOGRAPH BY BEN SCHNALL.

Under lighting conditions such as the above, there will also be shifts in the apparent brightness or reflectance of colors. This will be discussed in the following chapter.

The truth of Kruithof's principle may lie in man's heredity and experience with nature. No matter, reverse the conditions and eerie results will follow. Blue light *at dim levels* will give the world an ashen and ghostly aspect. Red or orange light *at high levels* will obviously cause distortions in surfaces and objects. The assumption that good color discrimination requires pure daylight (bluish) holds true at high levels of intensity only, not at low ones!

So for agreeableness and normality in illumination, it is proper to stay warm at low levels and go cooler, if desired, at high levels. This is the way the "psychology" of vision operates. No one "color temperature" holds throughout. Indeed, the temperature of the light source must "curve" from warm to cool as intensity is heightened. Also, some directional light should be introduced to create an interesting play of highlight and shadow. The beauty of three-dimensional form can be destroyed by too much "flat" lighting.

14 THE PHENOMENON OF COLOR CONSTANCY

Couple Kruithof's principle with what (with due apologies) I term Birren's principle and much about good balance in the control of color and brightness in the environment can be learned and put to effective use—particularly at moderate light levels.

To go now from illumination to color, clinical studies have revealed the need and importance of fairly uniform "values" (brightnesses) in the field of view. Here again recommended practices have been set forth by the lighting profession, though many of them are irritating to designers. The truth of the matter is that the technically ideal interior, approved by the engineer, may often be disliked when emotional judgment is called upon. The agreeable environment can be no fixed thing, for people do not think or feel the same about the same things. However, if the lighting engineer tends to be strict about light levels of illumination and uniformity of brightness, he is not entirely without justice on his side. If technical engineering may lead to monotony, much esthetic interior design may lead to needless and objectionable contrast.

There is wide latitude in the use of decorative colors, but even here objective factors cannot be ignored. The colors used for walls and furnishings in an interior are in a province definitely ruled by architects and designers who are schooled in esthetic knowledge that may be known to few lighting engineers. Little interference should be allowed to creative effort. However, there are limits to color use that certainly may profitably be regarded by the thoughtful designer.

It should never be naively assumed that critical seeing tasks merely need adequate light. The operation of the eye is largely muscular, and being muscular any excessive activity will tire it out—regardless of light levels or surrounding. Glare, prolonged convergence, constant shifts in accommodation, constant adjustments to extreme brightness differences, all involve wearisome muscular chores. (The retina, however, like the human brain, seems more or less immune to fatigue.)

In the main, and as far as color is concerned, brightness contrasts should not be unduly excessive, if the eye (and body) are to function comfortably and readily.

If the environment is to be stimulating and "outward" in its direction, high brightness and warmth of color may be desirable. If it is to be "inward" in its direction and conducive to thought and contemplation, less brightness and coolness of color may be preferred.

If human appearance is important, the light source should be warm, and background colors should not exceed approximately 50 or 55% reflectance — otherwise the phenomenon of brightness contrast may operate to give the skin an unfavorably dark pallor by direct visual comparison.

These are the highlights of sound practice. They refer, let me repeat, to conditions under which difficult eye tasks may be performed or where human welfare is of significant concern. In purely casual spaces, such as in homes, the designer can take a more relaxed view. No one will object to sitting in a dimly lit room unless called upon to look up a number in a telephone directory. At the other extreme, basking on a sunny beach may be pleasant for getting a coat of tan, but not for the glare that would accompany the reading of a book.

The chapters that follow will, with their relevant color charts, describe good practices in

MAN'S VISION HAS DEVELOPED UNDER NATURAL CONDITIONS. IT IS REMARKABLY VERSATILE AND WILL RESPOND EFFICIENTLY TO RADICALLY DIFFERENT DEGREES OF LIGHT INTENSITY AND COLOR TINT. PHOTOGRAPH BY H. ARMSTRONG ROBERTS.

THE INDOOR-OUTDOOR LIFE HAS BECOME PART OF THE AMERICAN SCENE. IT NECESSITATES CAREFUL ATTENTION TO A BALANCE OF NATURAL AND ARTIFICIAL LIGHT SOURCES, ALL OF WHICH HUMAN VISION CAN TAKE IN STRIDE. ORIGINAL DESIGN BY PAUL LASZLO. PHOTOGRAPH BY JULIUS SHULMAN.

the use of color for various types of interiors. They will also offer suggested standards which may be matched or approximated. And these colors, incidentally, are far from academic, being tried and proved in all cases for which they are prescribed.

Color constancy, the main topic of this chapter, is one of the most unusual and interesting of phenomena in human vision. It concerns the fact that the colors of the world will persist in having a "genuine" appearance under markedly different conditions of illumination in which they may be seen. In terms of intensity alone, for example, a white surface will remain white to the eye (and brain) whether seen in full daylight or in the dark recesses of a cellar—despite a variance in lighting intensity which may extend from 1,000 footcandles outdoors to one footcandle indoors. It is this amazing ability of the eye to accommodate itself to light that causes so much debate about light levels. The eye sees quite well at low intensities, reaches something of an optimum at from 30 to 50 footcandles, but continues to "hold its own" well up into 1,000 footcandles or more.

Within these same limits, colors would also remain normal, with exceptions which will be explained shortly.

Surprisingly enough, where colored or tinted light sources are introduced, color constancy still prevails. Few people are conscious of the effects of differences in light intensity and color tint during the course of a day. A white handkerchief does not turn gray when a cloud passes under the sun. The sunny side of a red barn looks quite similar in shade. Dawn and dusk may be warm and mellow, but nature keeps to a genuine appearance.

Color constancy is a natural endowment, known not only among men but among birds and beasts. Consider the following oddity. A white surface on a white or gray background, when showered with red light will still look white. It is, of course, no longer white but red, inasmuch as it actually transmits red energy into the eye. And this red color, which still looks white, may actually reflect more red than a truly red surface seen under white light!

What is vital to the phenomenon of color constancy is that *general* illumination must cover the whole field of view. This condition is probably necessary for vision to hold its judgment of the normal. Where a lighting engineer may show shadow boxes of different illumination sources (such as fluorescent) he is being unfair. A daylight fluorescent tube is obviously bluer than an incandescent bulb. The difference may indeed be quite pronounced when the two light sources are seen side by side. But if an entire room is illuminated with daylight fluorescent—or incandescent—no such consciousness of color tint will be experienced, thanks to color constancy.

In Kruithof's principle, previously described, the colors of an environment will appear normal (a) when the tint of the light source is warm at low levels, (b) yellowish at slightly higher levels, and (c) white or bluish at high levels. This is all natural to man's sense of vision. It means, in effect, that candlelight and incandescent light are suitable and quite natural for dim environments, while yellower, whiter and bluer illumination becomes equally suitable and natural as the intensity of the light source increases. Perhaps the reader has noted in his own experience that weak warm light (a candle, a lone incandescent bulb) does not have the weird effect of a bluish fluorescent light which is equally feeble. The fluorescent source will cast a ghoulish and cadaverous pale over its surroundings, human complexion included.

Now to Birren's principle. The great majority of architects, interior designers, and others who specify color for buildings, seem to be unaware of certain definite occurrences that take place *in the apparent brightness or value of colors* as illumination levels are varied from dim to bright. This is a phenomenon noted by many students of vision for it was given special attention by the great German psychologist, David Katz.

Despite the wonders of color constancy (the persistence of vision in seeing genuine color qualities under widely different conditions of light), the values of color undergo shifts when exposed to different degrees of light intensity. By the term *value*, the author refers to apparent brightness or reflectance.

Refer to an accompanying chart and consider the following.

1. As long as the eye is able to see, a white surface will always appear white—from under a fraction of a footcandle to high into the hundreds of footcandles.

2. In complete dark-adaptation, the eye loses *all sense* of color. This is because the cone endings of the retina, sensitive to color, grow dormant, and seeing is taken over by the color insensitive rods.

3. However, because near-darkness is seldom encountered in a decorative problem, the phenomena of complete dark-adaptation may be set aside.

4. Looking at a scale of gray values from white to black, the relationships of the steps will remain normal—one to the other—for *all* illumination levels above 25 or 30 footcandles.

HERE IS A VIEW OF THE ROOSEVELT ELEMENTARY SCHOOL IN WORCESTER, MASSACHUSETTS. UNDER BRIGHT ILLUMINATION—A NECESSARY CONDITION FOR GOOD VISION—COLOR VALUES WILL BE CLEARLY PERCEIVED. STRONG HUES MAY HAVE TO BE TONED SOMEWHAT TO AVOID GARISH EFFECTS. PHOTOGRAPH COURTESY HOLOPHANE COMPANY.

HUMAN VISION IS OFTEN CALLED UPON TO UNDERTAKE INCREDIBLY DIFFICULT TASKS, SUCH AS INDICATED IN THIS AIRCRAFT COCKPIT. HERE FINE DETAILS MUST BE DISCRIMINATED IN NEAR-DARKNESS. PHOTOGRAPH COURTESY SPERRY GYROSCOPE COMPANY.

5. Below 25 or 30 footcandles, however, there will be a pronounced contraction.

6. This is because, as illumination grows dim, all deep colors tend to "melt" together in value or brightness, if not in hue.

7. For example, under 30 or more footcandles of light, the mid or medium point (value) on a neutral scale will be judged as a gray having a reflectance of about 20 percent. Such a gray, under good light, will appear to be visually half-way between white and black.

Under 20 footcandles, the mid-step will require a reflectance of about 25 percent to appear half-way between white and black.

At 10 footcandles, the mid-step will require a reflectance of about 30 percent.

At 5 footcandles, the mid-step will require a reflectance of about 40 percent.

FOOTCANDLES OF ILLUMINATION

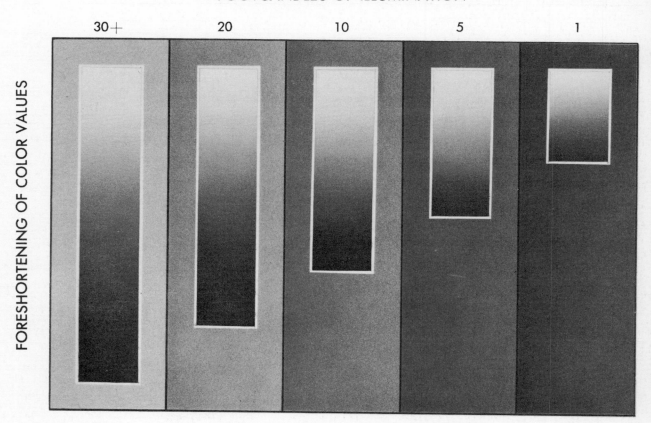

FORESHORTENING OF COLOR VALUES

30+ 20 10 5 1

THIS CHART SHOWS BIRREN'S PRINCIPLE. THE FORESHORTENING OF COLOR VALUES OR APPARENT LIGHTNESS UNDER DIFFERENT DEGREES OF ILLUMINATION INTENSITY IS ILLUSTRATED HERE. ALL VALUES FROM WHITE TO BLACK WILL BE FULLY CLEAR FOR ALL INTENSITIES ABOVE 30 FOOTCANDLES. UNDER LOWER INTENSITIES THE SCALES WILL APPEAR TO GROW SHORTER AND SHORTER FROM THE BOTTOM UP. THIS IS BECAUSE COLORS OF DEEP VALUE TEND TO MELT TOGETHER AND APPEAR ALIKE AS LIGHT GETS DIM. HOWEVER, WHITE ALWAYS REMAINS WHITE TO HUMAN PERCEPTION.

And at 1 footcandle, the mid-step will require a reflectance of about 45 or even 50 percent.

8. In brief, as light goes dim, the gray scale (a) gets shorter and shorter, *but from the bottom up*, and (b) all the dark tones below any judged mid-step will tend to blend together and appear alike in value or brightness. White alone will hold its constancy.

Many practical lessons may be learned from this phenomenon or principle. At the bottom, for example, in very dim light the true values of dark colors will be lost more or less completely. The U.S. Navy at one time used black

for the walls of submarine conning towers and combat information centers where near-darkness was necessary during battle operations. This standard has been changed to a medium green, and for a clear reason. When the eye is dark-adapted *any color reflecting 20 percent or less will appear black.* So why use black? After all, battle practice is infrequent on a naval vessel. Most of the time the lights are on. Personnel instead of being exposed to a black coffin of an interior can be surrounded by a pleasing green—with no sacrifice of functionalism in the color treatment of the interior.

There are other morals to this (Birren's)

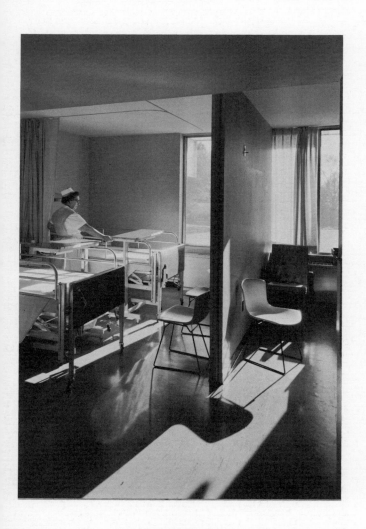

AS A MATTER OF PERSONAL TASTE, MOST PERSONS WILL PREFER A WARM LIGHT OF MODERATE INTENSITY—AND SUCH WOULD BE DESIRABLE FOR PATIENTS' FACILITIES IN A HOSPITAL. PHOTOGRAPH BY ALEXANDRE GEORGES.

principle. It is wholly incongruous to pick colors in bright light and expect them to appear the same under dim light. Again, if the environment is designed for soft light (a living room, a cocktail lounge, an exclusive restaurant, an enclosed setting or rest area), there is little sense in using dark colors. Dark colors, in fact, may "fall apart" and grow muddy. If the eye of an occupant in a dimly lit room is to sense and appreciate the colors of the decor in walls, floors, furnishings, *no color with a reflectance of less than 10 or 15 percent should be used.* Anything deeper may be meaningless—if not ugly because of the inability of the eye to perceive it clearly.

HIGH BRIGHTNESS AND HIGH-LEVEL ILLUMINATION WILL STIMULATE IMPULSE BUYING. THIS IS BECAUSE VISUAL AND MOTOR RESPONSES IN PEOPLE ARE ACTIVATED. PHOTOGRAPH SHOWS GREAT SCOTT SUPERMARKET IN PROVIDENCE, RHODE ISLAND. PHOTOGRAPH COURTESY HOLOPHANE COMPANY.

COLOR VALUES IN DECORATION MUST BE STUDIED WITH CARE IF THEY ARE TO MAKE VISUAL SENSE UNDER DIM ILLUMINATION. AN EXCELLENT JOB HAS BEEN DONE HERE. NOTE THE AVOIDANCE OF EXCESSIVELY DARK TONES. ORIGINAL DESIGN BY PAUL LASZLO. PHOTOGRAPH BY ROBERT C. CLEVELAND.

IN THE DIM ENVIRONMENT, SO RELAXING TO HUMAN MOODS, EXTREMELY DARK COLORS MAY NOT BE CLEARLY PERCEIVED. COLOR "VALUES" NEED TO BE ADJUSTED TO MEET THE LIGHTING CONDITIONS FOR WHICH THEY ARE INTENDED. PHOTOGRAPH COURTESY ARTHUR MORGAN, DESIGNERS.

15 PSYCHOPHYSICS IN HOSPITALS AND SCHOOLS

Now to the business of suggesting colors and specifications for institutional, industrial, and commercial establishments—interiors where beauty should be supplemented by purpose and utility. I realize that some designers may resist this sort of advice, general and liberal though it is in intention. The creative mind is supposed to be original and never to do the same thing twice. This may be a commendable ideal where high individuality is desired (as in homes), but it hardly applies to applications of color meant to serve the best interest and welfare of masses of people who have visual problems to be eased and solved.

After all, the creative designer may do what he wants anyhow. There are many others—architects, building superintendents and administrators, business men, painters — who may have less taste and skill and who will welcome help. In numerous instances, choice of color needs to be justified on more than a personal basis. With the subjects of this chapter, for example, hospital and school superintendents, committees, and boards may have to pass on color specifications. The more sense, order, and reason that can be put into the color plan, the more readily will it be accepted and the better will it serve functional ends.

It is my desire to build defenses for sound and meaningful uses of color and to pass on a sizable fund of experience and case history to support them. I have worked in all the fields included in this book. I have employed all the colors presented on the charts. I have further conducted many studies built on the best of scientific practice in vision, illumination, and clinical psychology. I would like to share the results of this work for the help and guidance it may offer to others.

The basic color problems encountered in hospitals and schools relate to many other fields, homes excepted for the most part. Efficient and comfortable vision are necessary, plus any possible psychological values conducive to human welfare—emotional relief for the student, speedy convalescence for the ill.

On the matter of visual comfort, let me offer a few comments on so-called "eyestrain." The human eye is a very durable organ. It expects to perform duties demanded by nature, and it will take much abuse. Some lighting engineers claim inimical effects from poor light. Some ophthalmologists say the eye can hardly be damaged in an effort to see. It is no more logical to speak of eyestrain from seeing than it is to speak of earstrain from hearing or legstrain from walking.

Eye fatigue—a better term—probably does not affect the eye itself so much as the organism in general. An effort to see in poor light—or to hear someone whisper—obviously does no damage. However, the whole organism may grow tense. Brows may furrow and muscles grow taut. Shortly the body is tired and may even experience headache and nausea.

Where there are conditions of undue brightness and glare, similar reactions are noted. Here, even if the retina of the eye is not degenerated, there is much evidence that other functions are affected. Such things as muscular imbalance, distortion of the lens due to taxed eye muscles may well result. While it may be true to state that the eye isn't damaged, it certainly may be thrown out of kilter.

But regardless of eye defects—if any—no one can argue over the matter of great dis-

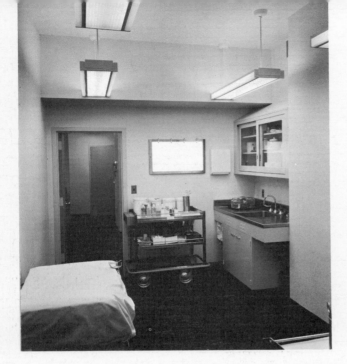

IN THE TREATMENT ROOM OF THE WORCESTER CITY HOSPITAL WALLS ARE PALE GREEN, CEILING WHITE, COUNTER BEIGE. FLOOR IS DARK BECAUSE OF HEAVY USAGE BY HOSPITAL STAFF AND PATIENTS. ISADORE AND ZACHARY ROSENFIELD AND E. TODD WHEELER, ARCHITECTS. PHOTOGRAPH BY GLINTENKAMP/PHOTOG. ASSOC.

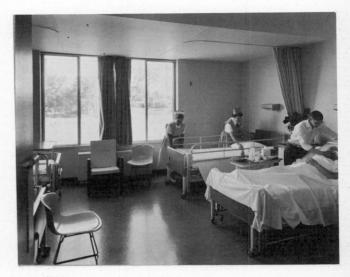

IN THE MEMORIAL HOSPITAL AT BELLEVILLE, ILLINOIS, WALLS ARE A WARM, FRIENDLY BEIGE AND THE FLOOR IS GRAY. VARIETY IS INTRODUCED IN DIFFERENT LOCATIONS THROUGH THE USE OF DRAPERIES AND BED CURTAIN SCREENS IN SUCH HUES AS YELLOW, TURQUOISE, SOFT ORANGE. ISADORE AND ZACHARY ROSENFIELD AND HELLMUTH, OBATA & KASSABAUM, ARCHITECTS. PHOTO-GRAPH BY ALEXANDRE GEORGES.

comfort and fatigue. To correct these would be enough in itself. Thus the need for ample light and minimum glare. Fairly uniform values of brightness in the field of view become desirable not only psychologically but physiologically as well.

In the case of hospitatals, enough research has been conducted in recent years to warrant a fairly rational specification of colors. Unfortunately, because human reactions to colors are emotional, clinical data are not easy to gather and facts are difficult to set forth. None the less, tendencies are strong enough in certain directions to justify a number of general if not specific conclusions.

It is commonly admitted today by many psychiatrists and clinical psychologists that color has one simple but clear effect: its emotional impact tends to lead to outwardly directed attention. In other words, it is diverting and pleasing. This in itself is good for any patient, for it may offer some relief, even if mi-

nor, from inner tensions. It has the same influence as any agreeable sensation, and in this it is at least helpful to recovery.

Still omitting any specific therapy for color, it would seem from the above generalities that a hospital color plan can be built upon intelligent elements and not left to mere chance or personal feeling. For example, there are some uses for color in the hospital which do not essentially concern beauty or emotion. In the surgery, the development of artificial light sources of high intensity more than a decade ago led to problems of glare which were to a large extent resolved in the use of special tones of blue-green on walls and furnishings. Such application of color reduced brightness in the field of view, built up better visual contrast, complemented the reddish tint of human blood and tissue, and thus aided the acuity of the surgeon's eyes. The factor of appearance was wholly incidental.

Visual comfort also applies to all service

THE ENVIRONMENT IN THE CHILDREN'S UNIT OF THE WORCESTER CITY HOSPITAL, WORCESTER, MASSACHUSETTS, IS APPROPRIATELY COLORFUL, WITH YELLOW ON CABINETS, CORAL ON CHAIRS, AND GENEROUS AREAS OF BRIGHT RED, GREEN, AND BLUE ON WALLS. COLUMNS ARE WHITE. ISADORE AND ZACHARY ROSENFIELD AND E. TODD WHEELER, ARCHITECTS.

SHADES IN THIS CLASSROOM AT DARIEN HIGH SCHOOL, DARIEN, CONNECTICUT, ARE GREENISH BLUE AND PROVIDE A PLEASING BUT UNOBTRUSIVE THEME. WALLS ARE LIGHT AQUA BLUE. FLOOR IS OFF-WHITE TILE FLECKED WITH BLUE. CABINETS ARE NATURAL WOOD. PHOTOGRAPH COURTESY J. STANLEY SHARP, ARCHITECT. PHOTOGRAPH BY GIL AMIAGA.

areas and accommodations for patients. Excessive contrasts should be avoided. In private rooms and wards, ceilings should perhaps be tinted because of the supine position of the bedridden guest. Wall areas and floors should be soft in tone, with a reflectance between 40 and 60 per cent. Furnishings and draperies should not be too pure in hue or too pronounced in design. Brilliant reds, yellows, and blues may be "pretty" enough to healthy persons, but they are unduly impulsive and may grow monotonous to a confined patient. Yet in parlors, solaria, and recreation areas, more freedom can be permitted and is, indeed, desirable for an interesting "change of pace."

It is obvious that as reason is brought to bear on the hospital color plan, variety automatically results, not as an end in itself, but as a result of purpose and function. This is the way things should be, for the hospital environment will be designed in a way that is individual to its needs and rightfully adapted to the high

IN THE TOKENEKE ELEMENTARY SCHOOL IN DARIEN, CONNECTI-
CUT, THERE IS GOOD NATURAL LIGHT AND THE SCHOOL IS WELL
DECORATED. WALLS ARE A NATURAL COLOR TO BALANCE INSIDE
AND OUTSIDE BRIGHTNESS. COLOR IS THEN INTRODUCED IN
GREEN FLOOR, TERRA COTTA SAILCLOTH ROOM DIVIDER, YELLOW
IN ADJACENT PATIO ENTRANCE. O'CONNOR AND KILHAM, ARCHI-
TECTS. PHOTOGRAPH BY JOSEPH W. MOLITOR.

IN THE LIBRARY AT COLGATE UNIVERSITY IN HAMILTON, NEW
YORK, WALLS ARE BEIGE, FLOOR IS CORK. DRAPERIES ARE OF
LINEN, PRINTED IN BRIGHT BLUE AND GREEN. UPHOLSTERY IS ALSO
BLUE AND GREEN. WHILE COLORFUL, THE SCHEME IS NON-DIS-
TRACTING. O'CONNOR AND KILHAM, ARCHITECTS. PHOTOGRAPH
BY JOSEPH W. MOLITOR.

purposes of medical care.

Refer now to Chart 12 (page 109) for recommended specifications. Note the selection of
colors; it is also appropriate to schools. Omitted
for hospital and school use are such colors as
blue, yellow-green and orchid (purple). Here
are the reasons.

While a spectral blue is a highly favored and
popular color—and excellent for other fields—
it tends to have a cold and bleak appearance
over long exposure. Also, being sharply re-
fracted by the eye, it tends to cause temporary
near-sightedness which is visually distressing
to many persons. It will be noted that the Teal
Blues on Chart 12 are on the green side.

Yellow-green (chartreuse) is the color of
sickness itself. While it may have "fashion"
interest, its visual and emotional associations
are unfavorable. Reflections from it give the
skin a "sickly" pallor. The same is more or less
true of shades of purple, violet, orchid, lilac—
which are more stylish than functional.

Now looking at Chart 12, consider these
suggestions.

Light Blue-Green and Medium Blue-Green
are particularly good hospital colors. They are
the direct complements of human complexion
and not only afford a flattering background
but cause pinkish after-images which give the
world a healthful glow.

For the surgery and adjacent facilities, consider Light Blue-Green, with Medium Blue-
Green in operating rooms. Ceiling in both areas
should be white.

Light Blue-Green, Light Warm Gray, or
Oyster White may be applied to service areas,
laboratories, sterilizing rooms, utility rooms,
diet kitchens.

In patients' accommodation, fairly soft
tones are better than "sharp" ones for the pur-

pose of greater subtlety and refinement. Since warm, bright colors *tend* to be exciting and to draw attention outward, they seem desirable for convalescent patients and for maternity sections. Here there would be good reason to consider Pink, Flesh, or Beige; they create subjective feelings which are more or less positive in nature. On the other hand, since cool, subdued colors *tend* to be subduing and to inspire a more relaxed mood, they are more suitable for chronic patients. Light Blue-Green, Light Teal Blue, and Light Green would be appropriate for such rooms.

Ceilings in private rooms and wards are best tinted. For this purpose, the wall color can be mixed in equal parts (50-50) with white to provide a ceiling tint.

End wall treaments are also suggested for private rooms and wards. Here deeper, harmonizing tones may be applied, though never on window walls. Consider such combinations as Light Blue-Green (three walls) with Medium Blue-Green (on one end or side wall); Pink with Rose; Light Teal Blue with Medium Teal Blue; Light Green with Medium Green.

Treatment rooms, X-ray, physiotherapy and the like may be Light Blue-Green, Light Green or Light Teal Blue. Adjacent dressing rooms—and toilets in general—are best in Pink or Flesh to reflect a pleasing glow.

Corridors and stairwells are suggested in Soft Yellow or Beige for a sunny effect.

Medium Warm Gray may be considered standard for miscellaneous trim or equipment.

In public spaces, lobbies, parlors, almost any of the colors on Chart 12 may be used—or the designer can depart from them as he wishes. Functionalism here is not too important as far as color is concerned.

As to schools, similar principles, as above,

A MULTI-PURPOSE ROOM AND CORRIDOR LIBRARY IN THE WINCHELL ELEMENTARY SCHOOL IN KALAMAZOO, MICHIGAN HAS WALLS OF YELLOW, GREEN, AND GOLD WITH TURQUOISE ACCENTS. PERKINS & WILL, ARCHITECTS-ENGINEERS, CHICAGO, ILLINOIS, STAPERT-PRATT-BULTHUIS-SPRAW-CROTHERS, ASSOCIATE ARCHITECTS. PHOTOGRAPH BY BILL ENGDAHL, HEDRICH-BLESSING.

AN ATTRACTIVE SCHOOL AREA IN THE INDIAN TRAIL ELEMENTARY SCHOOL IN HIGHLAND PARK, ILLINOIS, USED FOR MANY PURPOSES. THE ARCHES ARE NATURAL WOOD. WALL TONES ARE FAIRLY NEUTRAL WITH BRIGHT COLORS CONFINED TO STAGE CURTAINS. PERKINS & WILL, ARCHITECTS-ENGINEERS, CHICAGO, ILLINOIS. PHOTOGRAPH BY SUTER, HEDRICH-BLESSING.

may be followed. Most of the colors on Chart 12 are soft in tone and have been developed on good scientific principles to effect an ideal seeing condition.

In elementary grades and kindergartens, warm colors may be preferred, such as Pink, Flesh, Soft Yellow—or use different colors on different walls. The warm color is exciting to young minds and emotions and will relieve anxiety because of agreeable distraction.

In classrooms and study rooms, the cool color will aid concentration on books and lessons. Here good colors are Light Blue-Green, Light Teal Blue, Light Green.

End walls also serve a functional purpose in schools by reducing contrast in the forward field of view. Consider the following combinations, all using Light Warm Gray for side and back walls, but with the front end wall in Medium Blue-Green, Rose, Medium Teal Blue or Medium Green.

Soft Yellow or Oyster White would be excellent for corridors, locker rooms, gymnasiums, shops.

Laboratories would perhaps be best in Light Warm Gray or any of the light, cool colors. Almost any of the colors would be suitable for the domestic sciences. Washrooms could be Pink for girls and Light Teal Blue for boys.

Offices should preferably be cool in tone. Go easy with Oyster White, however, in any area where critical seeing tasks are likely to be encountered.

All ceilings in office areas, virtually without exception, should be plain white or off-white for good light reflection and for the reduction of shadows.

Consider Medium Warm Gray as a practical finish for miscellaneous equipment and also for trim, baseboards, radiator enclosures, machinery, bins, racks, etc.

Note: On the matter of food service for hospitals and schools, see special chapter at end of this book.

IN THE DEAN'S OFFICE AT THE UNIVERSITY OF DENVER LAW CENTER WARM AND NEUTRAL COLOR IS USED ON WALLS, CARPET, AND DRAPERIES. LEATHER CHAIRS ARE UPHOLSTERED IN BLACK. THE EFFECT IS QUIET AND REFINED. PERKINS & WILL, ARCHITECTS-ENGINEERS, CHICAGO, ILLINOIS, BUELL & COMPANY, ASSOCIATE ARCHITECT. PHOTOGRAPH BY BILL HEDRICH, HEDRICH-BLESSING.

THIS IS A VIEW OF THE AUDITORIUM AT BUTLER AREA SENIOR HIGH SCHOOL IN BUTLER, PENNSYLVANIA. ACCORDING TO THE ARCHITECTS, "SEATING FOR 1,198 VARIES FROM LIGHT, COOL YELLOWS AND BEIGES TO WARM, BRIGHT ORANGE, AND DEEP RICH BROWN, WITH SOFT, MELLOW GREEN OFFERING A CHANGE OF PACE." STAGE CURTAINS ARE BEIGE. PERKINS & WILL, ARCHITECTS-ENGINEERS, CHICAGO, ILLINOIS. HOWARD, BURT & HILL. ASSOCIATE ARCHITECTS. PHOTOGRAPH BY JOSEPH W. MOLITOR.

16 FUNCTIONALISM IN INDUSTRIAL PLANTS

There has been a considerable revolution in the functional decoration of industrial plants. Where once there was drab use of white, ivory, deep green, and "battleship" gray, brighter and more pleasing colors have entered the scene (a) to create a more uniform, comfortable, and efficient seeing environment, and (b) to add psychological interest for the workers and relief from monotony.

While the colors shown on Chart 12 for hospitals and schools are largely applicable to the industrial plant, certain other standards are recommended; these are presented on Chart 13 (page 111). Included are five brilliant hues for purposes of identification and safety.

As M. Luckiesh, a lighting authority has written, "A visual task is inseparable from its environment.... High visibility, ease of seeing and good seeing conditions are overwhelmingly the result of good brightness engineering." This means color.

What is variously known as functional color, color conditioning, and color dynamics, had its beginning in the mid-twenties of this century. At that time, studies were made in hospital operating rooms to lessen glare and improve the vision of the surgeon. For perhaps the first time, the use of color in an environment was considered from a point of view other than that of pure esthetics. Much research was undertaken and techniques were worked out to measure eye fatigue by instrumental means. Many of the principles developed have already been discussed. The point was firmly established that control of brightness and color in an interior had vital bearing on human efficiency and well-being.

After adaptation to hospitals and schools functional color was applied to industrial plants and offices to increase production, improve quality of workmanship and manual

THESE TWO PICTURES SHOW WHAT CAN BE ACCOMPLISHED WITH NEW LIGHTING AND A COAT OF PAINT. ALTHOUGH THERE IS BETTER APPEARANCE, FUNCTIONAL COLOR IS PRIMARILY CONCERNED WITH BETTER VISIBILITY, PRODUCTION, AND SAFETY. PHOTOGRAPH COURTESY U. S. GOVERNMENT PRINTING OFFICE, WASHINGTON, D. C.

COLOR PUTS NEATNESS AND ORDER INTO COMPLEX MECHANICAL LAYOUTS AND, AT THE SAME TIME, LESSENS GLARE AND CREATES AN EFFICIENT ENVIRONMENT. IN THIS INTERIOR, WALLS AND COLUMNS ARE A SOFT GREEN ON THE LIGHT SIDE, WITH THE FLOOR A MEDIUM GREEN. PHOTOGRAPH COURTESY WESTERN ELECTRIC COMPANY.

skill, reduce "seconds" and "rejects," cut down accident frequencies, raise standards of plant housekeeping and machine maintenance, reduce absenteeism, and improve labor morale.

Because the requirement of good scientific practice in the use of color has been set forth in other chapters, let me go directly to the matter of color specifications for factories. As mentioned, keep an eye on the chapter devoted to hospitals and schools and to Chart 13 which

refers specifically to industrial plants. Also consider the next chapter when the seeing problem relates to offices. Colors for food service have been separately treated (Chapter XX).

For the most part, industrial overheads and ceilings should be white. Pale Green is sometimes recommended in this application and is often satisfactory. However, factory ceilings are frequently above the worker's normal field of view and therefore may not be a source of glare. White here will assure the maximum reflection of light to improve illumination and reduce shadows. If there is extensive steel—beams and trusses — plus composition roof decking, Light Gray as on Chart 13 may be used in lieu of white and will simplify painting. One disadvantage of a color tint on overhead is that it may prove to be an emotional distraction and may draw attention up and away from working levels.

Upper walls (generally to a line level with the bottom of roof beams or trusses) should have a reflectance between 50 and 60 per cent if floor and equipment are on the dark side, or between 60 and 70 per cent if such areas and surfaces in the interior are (or can be made) fairly bright. Wall brightnesses higher than 70 per cent are generally undesirable because of possible glare. However, they are allowable if there is excellent illumination and if all major surfaces are also pale.

If a dado is required to conceal stains, the color tone may be deeper than the walls. Floors should reflect if practical, 20 percent or more. Machinery and equipment should also be in the medium range.

Certain other refinements may be introduced. Window sashes should be white or light gray to lessen contrast with outside brightness. Machinery can have important parts highlighted in a pale color—such as Spotlight Buff on Chart 13—to reflect more light at significant parts and concentrate the worker's attention.

End wall treatments in medium tones have widespread application. Where many workers may be engaged at difficult tasks and may be so oriented as to face in the same direction, the end wall in a medium tone will help to overcome an unfavorable constriction of the pupil of the eye. Upon glancing up, the medium tone will afford relaxation rather than the stimulation of glare. It will likewise reduce the strain of prolonged convergence of the eyes and be psychologically pleasing.

VIEW OF MODERN PLANT OF ROYAL McBEE CORPORATION, SPRINGFIELD, MISSOURI. WALLS AND OVERHEAD ARE WHITE; NOTE LIGHTNESS OF FLOOR. A SOFT, UNIFORM BRIGHTNESS IN THE WORKER'S FIELD OF VIEW WILL ASSURE COMFORTABLE VISION WITH MINIMUM FATIGUE. FINE DETAILS WILL BE CLEARLY DISTINGUISHED. PHOTOGRAPH BY MIGNARD.

IN THE TURBINE ROOM OF CONNECTICUT LIGHT & POWER COM-
PANY, FLOOR IS RED QUARRY TILE. WALLS ARE YELLOW GLAZED
BRICK. CEILING IS BLUE. TURBINES ARE WHITE WITH SOME YELLOW.
KAHN & JACOBS, ARCHITECTS. PHOTOGRAPH BY EZRA STOLLER
ASSOCIATES.

As already discussed for hospitals and schools, the bright environment—using light colors—draws attention outward. It provides an ideal setting for vigorous and muscular tasks, or where there is considerable movement within an interior. The bright environment will keep people alert.

On the other hand, softer wall tones will be suitable for more sedentary occupations and will aid visual and mental concentration on localized tasks.

Refer now to the colors on Chart 13 which are suggested for industrial plants. Note that most of the standards are soft in tone. This is deliberate and meant to establish a non-distracting environment as well as practicality in maintenance by having better resistance to soiling. (Light and Medium Green, Soft Yellow, and Beige are the same as on the hospital and school chart.)

Green is a restful and natural-looking color for average factory interiors. It can be made

IN THIS IMMACULATE PLANT, THE CEILING IS WHITE, FLOOR LIGHT
MAPLE IN NATURAL FINISH. WALLS AND COLUMNS ARE A COOL
GREEN. MACHINERY IS BLUE-GRAY. MOVING PARTS OF THE OVER-
HEAD CONVEYOR ARE BRIGHT ORANGE TO ATTRACT ATTENTION.
PHOTOGRAPH COURTESY R. J. REYNOLDS TOBACCO COMPANY,
WINSTON-SALEM, NORTH CAROLINA.

to serve most purposes. Light Green (Chart 13) with Medium Green for dado is suggested —or Light Green for side and back walls, with Medium Green for end walls faced by most employees.

Beige and Sandalwood (as wall and dado, or wall and end wall) might be applicable to industrial interiors deprived of good natural light, located on courts, or with operations in which temperatures may be on the chilly side. The warmth of the tones will offer psycholog-ical compensation.

Light Blue and Medium Blue (again as wall and dado, or wall and end wall) may be speci-fied for a "cool" effect for plants in sunny re-gions or where temperature conditions tend to be unduly high.

In large, vaulty spaces, Soft Yellow may be combined with Medium Gray for dado. While Soft Yellow is high in brightness, the large in-teriors and far distances will in themselves overcome the hazard of glare.

In relatively small industrial areas with low ceilings the end wall scheme is a good one to prescribe. Here side and back walls (including window walls) may be Light Gray for proper control of brightness and a uniform level of eye adaptation. End walls could then be in Medium Green, Medium Blue, or Soft Yellow (where light may be dim).

White is not recommended for factory walls, except in areas having low occupancy, such as storage. For corridors and stairwells are recommended Soft Yellow upper walls with Medium Gray dado, stairs, and railings.

Medium Gray (or Medium Green) is proposed for machinery, equipment, racks, bins, shelving and the like. Machinery may be highlighted with Spotlight Buff applied to important areas where the worker's attention is to be concentrated. Deep Gray on Chart 13 should be restricted only to equipment where there is excessive exposure to dirt or oil. It should otherwise be avoided.

Washroom facilities could be of Aqua and Turquoise as in hospitals and schools (Chart 12). Rest rooms, lounges and recreation rooms could be in any of the colors found on Charts 13 or 12.

Finally, the safety colors of Chart 13 should by all means be utilized. These colors are part of a code originally developed by the author in 1942-3. First offered by du Pont, the code was approved by the National Safety Council in 1944, adopted in part by the American Standards Association in 1945 and more fully in 1953. Presented at a world congress on safety in Rome, 1955, it is now internationally recognized. It has been mandatory practice with the U.S. Navy since 1948.

In a functionally designed factory, bright colors are completely avoided for any decorative purposes; they would be irrelevant and hazardous because of high impulse attraction. However, where the brilliant color is used to direct attention, it serves the purpose of safety.

In applying the code, Solar Yellow (Chart 13)—by itself or with alternate black bands—is standard to mark strike-against, stumbling,

MACHINERY IS A LIGHT, COOL GRAY WHICH ENCOURAGES HIGH STANDARDS OF PLANT HOUSEKEEPING AND YET IS EASY ON THE EYES. NOTE HOW PRODUCTS (CIGARETTES) ARE DRAMATIZED. PHOTOGRAPH COURTESY R. J. REYNOLDS TOBACCO COMPANY, WINSTON-SALEM, NORTH CAROLINA.

bumping, or falling hazards. It is painted on obstructions, low beams, dead ends, the edges of platforms and pits, on curbing, posts, pillars, dangerous projections. Being the color of highest visibility in the spectrum, it is conspicuous under all lighting conditions.

Alert Orange is standard for acute hazards likely to cut, crush, burn, or shock the worker. It is painted around the edges of cutting knives and rollers. On the inside areas of machine guards and switch boxes it becomes a conspicuous reminder that such equipment should be protected. Here is the color of highest visual impact and well adapted to these purposes.

Fire Red is reserved entirely and exclusively for the marking of fire protection devices. The old use of red as a token of danger should be abandoned. (Incidentally, from 8 to 10 percent of men are partially blind to red.) The color is painted on walls behind extinguishers, on floors to prevent obstruction, on valves and fittings for fire hose connections.

Safety Green is standard to identify first aid equipment, cabinets for stretchers, gas masks,

medicines and the like.

Caution Blue is standard as a caution signal. It is placed as a symbol on equipment, elevators, machines, tanks, ovens, etc., cut down for repair. It may be used on switch control boxes as a silent reminder to the worker to make sure that his machine is clear before he operates it.

A further color code standard, not shown on Chart 13, is Radiation Purple. This, in the form of a propeller target on a yellow ground, is used to mark dangerous radioactive materials and radiochemicals. It is employed on doors, containers, labels, chests and the like to warn and instruct against exposure.

White, gray, or black are standard for aisle marks, waste receptacles, and relatively safe and unimportant things.

(Note. The following three color codes may be consulted. All are available from the American Standards Association, New York: Safety Color Code, Standard Z53.1-1953; Piping Identification, Standard A13-1928; Gray Finishes for Industrial Applications and Equipment, Standard Z55.1-1950.)

MACHINERY IN THIS PLANT IS GRAY, HIGHLIGHTED WITH BUFF ON IMPORTANT PARTS. WALLS ARE BLUE-GREEN. A SAFETY CODE, USING BRILLIANT ORANGE AND YELLOW, IS USED TO MARK HAZARDS. VIEW SHOWS MACHINE SHOP OF NEW YORK TRADE SCHOOL. PHOTOGRAPH COURTESY DU PONT.

17 COMFORT AND EFFICIENCY IN OFFICES

Let us devote a few more paragraphs to illumination. This time, however, the reader should accept my comments with a few grains of salt. Physical, mental, and emotional effects for color have occupied my interest for some years. I have written two books on the subject and a good number of articles for the medical press. Progress in the development of artificial light sources has been quite rapid—so fast, indeed, that biological and physiological studies of it have been pressed to keep up.

John Ott who has done much experimental work with plants, animals, light, and color, makes this summary: "Life on this earth has developed in response to the full spectrum of natural sunlight, and variations in the wavelength distribution produced by artificial light sources . . . seem to result in variations from normal growth development in both plants and animals."

The lighting profession by and large has been concerned with degrees of light intensity —any kind of white-appearing light—and little concerned with the spectral quality of such light. Average fluorescent light sources, for example, emit band spectra. That is, the color energy they send forth is not continuous as with sunlight and skylight but has gaps or bands. (See accompanying figures.)

One wonders if light that is incomplete, selective, and non-continuous in spectral distribution—so common to offices these days— has or will have unanticipated effects of one kind or another on human beings.

Biological effects from radiation have an impressive literature. Plants, for example, seem most reactive to red and blue and not at all to green. Animals show equally curious reactions. To refer to but a few recent observations, yellow light has been found to foster a high percentage of female guppies, while blue light apparently destroyed females. Laying

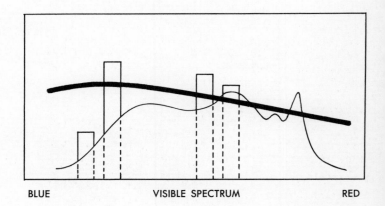

BLUE   VISIBLE SPECTRUM   RED

THE HEAVY LINE INDICATES A COOL WHITE TINT OF ABOUT 6500° AS MIGHT BE SEEN IN NATURAL LIGHT. NOTE THE CONTINUOUS (BUT CURVED) EMISSION THROUGHOUT THE SPECTRUM. THE LIGHT LINE INDICATES A FLUORESCENT LAMP OF SIMILAR WHITE APPEARANCE. THE VERTICAL BANDS INDICATE BASIC DISCHARGE FROM MERCURY VAPOR. WHILE THE TWO ILLUMINATIONS MAY LOOK ALIKE THEY ARE DIFFERENT IN COMPOSITION.

hens tend to produce infertile eggs under pink fluorescent but not under daylight fluorescent. When chinchillas were exposed to bluish fluorescent, mostly females were born; under incandescent light, mostly males were born. The same has happened with mice. According to one investigation, daylight produced a 50-50 ratio of male and female mice. Under bluish fluorescent, the result was 70 percent female and 30 percent male. Under pink fluorescent, the result was 30 percent females and 70 percent males.

One scientific acquaintance of the author has wondered—not without cause—if the exposure of children and adults to different qualities of illumination might not have serious effects on physical well-being and personality. Would little boys become girlish under persistent exposure to bluish light? Do unbalanced light sources lead to biological disturbances?

These points are brought up—with salt—to

VARIETY IN DESIGN, COLOR, TEXTURE ARE ALL SIGNIFICANT IN OFFICE PLANNING AND ASSURE RELIEF FROM MONOTONY DURING COURSE OF PUBLIC OR EMPLOYEE TRAFFIC. RICHARD J. NEUTRA, ARCHITECT. PHOTOGRAPH BY JULIUS SHULMAN.

A DEPARTMENT RECEPTION AREA OF THE NEW YORK LIFE INSUR-
ANCE COMPANY FOR WHICH FABER BIRREN DEVELOPED THE COLOR
PLAN FOR ALL FACILITIES. THIS AREA HAS BEIGE CARPET, MEDIUM
BLUE WALL BACK OF RECEPTIONIST, LIGHT BLUE UPHOLSTERY.
DRAPERIES ARE MULTICOLOR. PHOTOGRAPH BY J. WALKER GRIMM.

TICKET OFFICE OF PAKISTAN INTERNATIONAL AIRLINES AS SEEN
FROM STREET. FLOOR IS GREEN TERRAZZO WITH WHITE CIRCLE
DESIGN. WALLS ARE WHITE, CEILING SKY BLUE. REAR WALL FEA-
TURES COMPOSITION IN TEAK, WITH BRONZE MAP. COURTESY,
SPACE DESIGN GROUP, M. B. AFFRIME, DIRECTOR. PHOTOGRAPH
BY BERNARD LIEBMAN.

emphasize the point that there may be a lot more to light than merely greets the eye superficially. Fortunately, "true light" sources, containing a full gamut of the spectrum, are being developed and are currently available. (One of them is the Verilux system.) It is unquestionably sound to conclude that if the human organism has evolved during eons of time under the spectral quality of natural light, it ought to be given the same qualities of illumination in artificial sources. If it is not, results may be unfortunate.

Now to specifications for offices. At this writing, white and off-white are the current fashion for office decoration. If human knowledge of the requirements for a good seeing condition are to be respected, this rage for white is quite wrong; it is, in fact, inimical to human comfort and welfare. The practice should be abandoned—and quickly!

Let me give two quotations. M. Luckiesh writes, "It may be concluded that brightnesses somewhat lower than those of the central field are most desirable. All experimental evidence indicates that peripheral brightnesses higher than those of the central field are definitely undesirable." More direct and warning of trouble is the conclusion of C. E. Ferree and Gertrude Rand, both eminent in the field of ophthalmology: "The presence of high brilliances in the field of view produces a strong incentive for the eyes to fixate and accommodate for them, which incentive must be controlled by voluntary effort. The result of this opposition of voluntary control against strong reflex incentive is to tire the eye quickly and make it lose the power to sustain the precision of adjustment needed for clear seeing of the work.... High brightness in the field of view, if isolated from the task, may cause disruption. The eye will therefore struggle to set things right. *This striving to clear up its vision by ineffectual maladjustments is the cause of what is commonly called eyestrain."*

There is little question but that the decoration of an office should have functional elements and should respect recognized scientific practice. To look upon it as a strict problem in esthetics may lead to unanticipated trouble. Black desks in white interiors may be quite striking on casual inspection (some decorators have this penchant) but the attempt of a secretary or executive to perform a day's work may ruin his (or her) disposition, be harmful to the eye, and lead to a hurried trip to an eye doctor. Cases like this are encountered all too frequently.

Colors for offices can be rather cleaner and lighter than those for industrial and institutional purposes. They can also be more fashionable, being usually exposed to healthy adults and not essentially to patients or students. This is evident in the recommended palette of Chart 14 (page 113). Here is some preliminary guidance.

Office ceilings are best in white or off-white for good light reflection and to reduce contrast with the brightness of overhead lighting.

Off-white is *not* recommended for walls in working spaces. It may be satisfactory for corridors, closets, and storage areas, but not where critical seeing tasks are undertaken. (There is no off-white on Chart 14. For a suitable specimen, refer to Chart 12.)

For reasons already mentioned in the case of hospitals and schools, Chart 14 does not contain a light spectral blue—and one is not recommended. A medium blue, however, identified as Sapphire Blue, is approved for end walls or accent purposes.

IN THIS EXECUTIVE OFFICE IN THE IBM DATA CENTER, PHILADELPHIA, PENNSYLVANIA, REAR WALL IS NATURAL CORK, CARPET BEIGE, DRAPERIES CHARCOAL AND GRAY STRIPE. CHAIRS ARE UPHOLSTERED IN BLACK OR YELLOW. CARL J. PETRILLI, ARCHITECT. PHOTOGRAPH BY BEN SCHNALL.

IN THIS GENERAL OFFICE IN THE IBM DATA CENTER, PHILADELPHIA, PENNSYLVANIA, WALLS ARE A LIGHT NEUTRAL. FLOOR IS GRAY STREAKED WITH WHITE. DESKS ARE CHARCOAL GRAY WITH OFF-WHITE TOPS. WALL DECORATION AT RIGHT IS OF ROSEWOOD, WALNUT, SILVER LEAF, AND GOLD LEAF. CARL J. PETRILLI, ARCHITECT. PHOTOGRAPH BY BEN SCHNALL.

Nor does the office Chart 14 show deep colors. None has a reflectance of less than about ten percent. If deep colors are avoided in the office plan, there will be no danger of setting up severe brightness contrasts to tax the eye. Comfort—and visual efficiency—will be built-in, so to speak. Some designers may disagree, but office color scheming is not an exclusive problem in esthetics. It can (and should) be "good looking," of course, but it should also regard intelligent scientific practice as to what constitutes a proper seeing environment. Too much brightness, too much contrast, can impair visual performance, lead to optical and physical distress, and hence reduce the productive capacity of personnel.

Chart 14 contains only three colors that have been included before in this section: Light Warm Gray, Beige and Soft Yellow. All the rest are new at this point and individually chosen for office use.

Good basic wall tones are Sandtone, Light Warm Gray, Light Jade, Light Coral, Aqua, Beige, and Sprout Green. These may be applied with room orientation in view (warm colors for north and east exposures, cool colors for south and west), but it would perhaps be better to think in terms of work tasks. Large general offices where there is much activity might be functionally right in the warm tones. On the other hand, sedentary tasks requiring greater than normal visual and mental concentration will be aided with cool tones.

The author strongly favors the use of end walls in medium tones, both for general and private offices. Here the schemes may be tone-on-tone, such as Light Jade with Medium Jade, Light Coral with Medium Coral, Aqua with Turquoise, Beige with Cocoa, Sprout Green with Fern Green.

On another principle, major walls may be the same throughout adjacent facilities. For example, Sandtone or Light Warm Gray may be used as key tones, with accent colors on far end walls in any of the following: Medium Jade, Medium Coral, Turquoise, Cocoa, Fern Green, Soft Yellow, Sapphire Blue. Ordinarily it is best *not* to apply the fuller tones to window walls—nor to glass-paneled partitions.

Hyacinth and Sunset Orange, at the bottom of Chart 14, may be considered special. Their use should not be excessive. In corridors, one wall could be Sandtone or Light Warm Gray, and the opposite wall could be Soft Yellow, Sunset Orange or Hyacinth.

Most of the colors on Chart 14 have been chosen with general offices and work areas in mind. Private offices can be more decorative, and other colors not shown here can be considered for the satisfaction of more personal

IN THIS KEY-PUNCH ROOM, OF THE HERTZ CORPORATION IN NEW YORK, CEILING IS WHITE. MACHINES ARE SLATE GRAY, DRAPERIES WHITE. HOWEVER, CARPET IS A FAIRLY PURE BLUE-GREEN. DESIGNS FOR BUSINESS, INC., DESIGNERS. PHOTOGRAPH BY BEN SCHNALL.

THIS OFFICE AREA OF INTERNATIONAL MINERALS & CHEMICAL CORPORATION IN HOUSTON, TEXAS, IS EXTREMELY COLORFUL. WALL AT RIGHT IS MEDIUM BLUE. FLOOR IS OFF-WHITE. DRAPERIES ARE ORANGE AND WHITE. UPHOLSTERED CHAIRS ARE A GOLDEN YELLOW. BYERS-CLARK, INTERIOR PLANNING CONSULTANTS.

IN THIS GENERAL OFFICE AT THE HERTZ CORPORATION, NEW YORK, WALLS ARE IVORY, WITH PARTITION PANELS IN VARIOUS SHADES OF ORANGE AND YELLOW. FLOOR IS A GRAY AND BROWN MIXTURE. DESKS ARE GRAY WITH PANELS IN ORANGE OR YELLOW AS ON PARTITIONS. DESIGNS FOR BUSINESS, INC., DESIGNERS. PHOTOGRAPH BY BEN SCHNALL.

THIS GENERAL OFFICE OF INTERNATIONAL MINERALS & CHEMICAL CORPORATION IN HOUSTON, TEXAS, IS WELL LIGHTED, HAS PALE GRAY WALLS. THE FLOOR PATTERN IN STRIPES OF WHITE, GREEN, AND BLUE IS MATCHED IN THE FLOOR-LENGTH DRAPERIES AT THE REAR. BYERS-CLARK, INTERIOR PLANNING CONSULTANTS.

taste. The same applies to furnishings. Floors, however, are best on the light side for good reflection of illumination.

As to office equipment—desks, cabinets, files—the author would suggest medium to light tones, preferably neutral. He has designed an Optical Gray for this purpose which approximates the brightness of Medium Warm Gray on Chart 12. Desk tops could be a trifle lighter. Working surfaces in white may be attractive on casual sight, but they may cause glare, constrict the pupil opening of the eye and lower visual acuity. A medium or light gray (or green or beige), on the other hand, will serve as an ideal visual "cushion." It will hold the eye to a steady adjustment and lessen visual "shock" as a worker glances to lighter and darker areas in the environment.

PUBLIC ACCEPTANCE IN STORES

In retail stores colors may go brighter and cleaner than for hospitals, schools, industrial plants, and offices. Visual comfort and relief from fatigue are not of primary concern. Despite this, however, "functionalism" is to be taken into account. In the instance of stores, the color emphasis shifts from the physiological to the more or less emotional—to colors of high visibility, colors that command attention, have unquestionable mass appeal, and have been researched in terms of public acceptance.

Once again, I avoid matters of taste and personal opinion in favor of a less subjective approach. But I speak from considerable experience. To state my viewpoint simply, a well coordinated store—in terms of color—is primarily concerned with the wants and desires of the public. As every experienced retailer understands, good merchandising is not a matter of whim or personal opinion. In consumer goods, *right* colors sell in profitable volume, while *wrong* colors lie dormant in unsold and costly inventories.

In store decoration and lighting, every retail outlet is a "package" which must be sold to the public. Good colors appeal on sight, invite traffic, draw from competition, and otherwise serve economic (not merely artistic) ends in modern business. Let store appearance be drab, let it be too old or too high fashion, and the customer may turn on his (or her) heel and shop elsewhere.

In stores which are dedicated and devoted to the sale of merchandise to the public at large, color is a temperamental thing to handle correctly. Do not make the mistake of holding that color for the sake of color holds any particular magic.

If a drab store can be criticized, so too may an overstyled one. Human eyes and emotions are discriminating. The best gadget in the world will be rejected if its color doesn't suit popular fancy. And in the same way, the most friendly store in a neighborhood will be shunned if its decorative impression isn't inviting. If it may be granted that a washing machine, a kitchen mixer or a package wouldn't

IN THIS VIEW OF A WOMEN'S SPECIALTY SHOP, FLAH & CO. IN ROCHESTER, NEW YORK, WALLPAPER IS IN VIOLET AND WHITE; CARPET IS ALSO VIOLET. CEILING AND COUNTERS ARE OFF-WHITE. MORRIS KETCHUM, JR. AND ASSOCIATES, ARCHITECTS. PHOTOGRAPH BY ALEXANDRE GEORGES.

sell too well in tones of purplish mauve or mustard yellow, it may be equally granted that a store which has such colors on its walls would turn many a customer away in other directions.

It is unreasonable to subject store decoration to personal whims. Some designers make the mistake of thinking that to be different is to be wise. If this hardly applies to merchandise—which every business man knows—why should the store designer hold any such illusions? Customers are no different in their attitude toward the general atmosphere of a store than they are to the things the store sells. Subconsciously a woman may not expect to find the colors she likes (in merchandise) in a store that makes a display (on walls) of the colors she dislikes.

There are emotional reasons and "functional" reasons why certain colors are better than others. To begin with, the most liked colors in the psychological sense are blue, red and green. (Yellow may also be accepted for its high visibility and compulsion.) These primary hues, and tints of them, thus become good colors for walls, end walls, fixtures, displays. They appeal on sight, for they are universally enjoyed by all age levels and by persons of all races and cultural backgrounds.

Recommended color standards for stores are on Chart 15 (page 115). There are no duplicates of any of the colors previously shown in this second section of the book. Note the clean quality of the pastels and their bright partners. There are two fairly vivid and fashionable hues, Pastel Orange and Lime Green.

There are also four dark colors. In store decoration where eye fatigue is not a significant factor, sprightly contrast is in proper order. It is questionable, however, if too much white should be used, except on ceilings and over-

IN THE DOROTHEA PHARMACY IN EASTCHESTER, NEW YORK, WALLS ARE A WARM, LIGHT GRAY, WITH WHITE FIXTURES AND GOLD DETAILING. AN OVAL GOLD CARPET IS REPEATED IN A GOLD CEILING. THERE IS BRIGHT CONTRAST AND GREAT VISUAL INTEREST. COPELAND, NOVAK AND ISRAEL, ARCHITECTS.

head. Where there may be a high level of illumination—encountered in so many modern stores—large expanses of white may constrict the pupil opening of the eye, causing merchandise to appear dull and blurred. The inevitable "pull" of brightness may, with white, draw attention up and away from the products to be sold. Emphasis would be in the wrong place.

White, however, is in fashion these days and some use of it—as a foil for pastels and bright colors—can be dramatic. By itself it may hold little appeal, but it is clean-looking, luminous, and where it sets off chromatic hues it is quite effective. Colors themselves never clash with it.

Now to get down to cases. By and large, the pastel colors on Chart 15 are suggested for upper walls, while the bright colors may be used for backgrounds and displays in more direct line with the customer's vision. The deep colors are for accent. Under the assumption that the larger store has decorative talent available, my only presumption will be to suggest consideration of these standards. (Some of them have been used by one of the biggest "chains" in America.) Let me clarify.

An exclusive shop catering to an exclusive clientele can advisedly be quite unusual, fashionable, and stylish, depending on the taste of the owner and his designer. Any or all colors could be used with good judgment.

As already mentioned, however, if the store or shop caters to average public, overstyling may be hazardous. Many an establishment has made this mistake and regretted it. The taste of the masses is simple, but it is good taste. It is direct, frank, and honest. In glorifying the colors most persons like few chances are taken. In a package, for example, research has proved that poor colors will cause a drop in sales. The

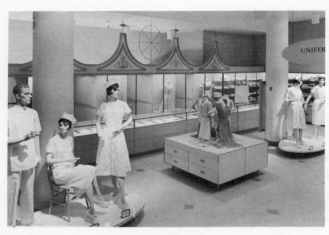

IN THE SPECIAL UNIFORM DEPARTMENT AT MACY'S, NEW YORK, WALLS AND COLUMNS ARE IN TONES OF AQUA, WITH DEEPER TURQUOISE FOR ACCENTS. FLOOR IS BEIGE. EFFECT IS COOL AND DRAMATICALLY COMPLEMENTS PRODUCTS ON DISPLAY. COPELAND, NOVAK AND ISRAEL, ARCHITECTS.

store is also a package, and its colors are vital.

Therefore, the colors of Chart 15, all of which rank high in research studies of color preference, may serve as a basis for the development of store color plans.

As alternate wall colors, more subdued in nature, use can also be made of Sandtone, Light Warm Gray, and Beige. These are shown on Chart 14.

How much color and how many colors? This will depend on circumstances and class of trade. Some stores make a practice of using a light color as a major theme. This color—generally an off-white—is then given contrast with areas of brighter hues in various locations. For example, a color like Blossom Pink may be used back of children's apparel or products. Sky Blue or Sea Blue may be used for men's wear. Pastel Canary or Bright Canary may be used for impulse merchandise, hard goods and the like.

Pastel Emerald and Bright Emerald are good all-round colors. However, Pastel Peacock and Bright Peacock are highly recommended for women's wear. This hue is the direct complement of human complexion. A woman trying on a dress will thus see herself at her best in the mirror.

If departments are set apart through the use of such different colors and if an off-white neutral is used as a foil there will be assurance of high attraction and emotional appeal, plus interesting variety to invite greater store traffic.

Yet too much brilliant color should be avoided. It should be used with purpose to direct the eye to locations where selling is to be done. Particularly intense colors like Pastel Orange and Lime Green can be spotted at the far end of stores to "pull" customers in toward

NOTE THE DIRECTIONAL LIGHT SOURCES IN THE SHOWROOM OF WILBURT, INC., NEW YORK. THESE BRING OUT THE PLASTIC FORM OF THE MERCHANDISE. MOST WALLS ARE WHITE FOR STRONG CONTRAST. FOR RELIEF, HOWEVER, DEEP BLUE AND PURPLE ARE APPLIED TO WALL AND COUNTER PANELS, BRIGHT PASTEL BLUE TO CEILING AT REAR, AND YELLOW TO STRAPS WHICH SUPPORT GLASS SHELVES. SPACE DESIGN GROUP, M. B. AFFRIME, DIRECTOR, DESIGNERS. PHOTOGRAPH BY BERNARD LIEBMAN.

these areas.

The deep tones of Chart 15, Forest Green, Walnut Brown, Maroon, Marine Blue, are suggested for display areas directly back of merchandise, not for upper walls or wide expanses. The deep tones will build up effective contrast with merchandise, set it off dramatically and generally contribute to a sprightly effect (a condition, incidentally, objectionable in offices, schools or hospitals, but appropriate to stores).

In stores and shops devoted to women, Emerald and Pink are good. For men there is good strategy in Blue and Canary. Similarly, cool colors in hot climates and the warm colors in cool climates will provide a measure of psychological color conditioning to interiors.

For fixtures, counters, tables, the author favors light neutral tones, such as Sandtone, Light Warm Gray, and Beige, to be found on Chart 14. Real or simulated woods are also suitable, but should also be on the light side. Where the fixture is immediately adjacent to merchandise, color conflict should be avoided. In simple terms, use the bright color to bring the customer to the products, and then let the fixture, counter, or table top be light in tone to provide direct local contrast.

For point of purchase areas, do not neglect texture. Warm wood tones may be desirable in men's and women's fashions, shoes, and the like. Dull textures will complement shiny and glittering products. Lustrous textures will enhance soft goods. The eye, remember, is sensitive to texture as well as color. Good display designers will introduce novelty and will work with all manners of things from fish nets to sea shells, from brass lamps to glass globes, from driftwood to balloons—all to excite the senses and ring the bells of cash registers.

Lastly, lighting is of tremendous impor-

IN THE CHILDREN'S WEAR DEPARTMENT OF GOLDWATERS, SCOTTS-DALE, ARIZONA, A CHILD'S WORLD HAS BEEN CREATED WITH BRIGHT COLORS AND INTERESTING DETAILS. A SPECIAL FEATURE IS THE OVERHEAD CANOPY MADE OF ALUMINUM AND ITALIAN PRISM GLASS WHICH SPARKLES WITH LIGHT. ORIGINAL DESIGN BY PAUL LASZLO. PHOTOGRAPH BY ROBERT C. CLEVELAND.

IN THIS LINGERIE DEPARTMENT AT GOLDWATERS, SCOTTSDALE, ARIZONA, THE THEME COLORS ARE PINK AND BEIGE. THESE ARE USED ON WALLS, FIXTURES, AND FLOORING. FULL-LENGTH MIRRORS, WHICH ECHO PATTERN OF ADJACENT WALLPAPER TO LEFT, ADD A FEMININE TOUCH. ORIGINAL DESIGN BY PAUL LASZLO. PHOTOGRAPH BY ROBERT C. CLEVELAND.

tance. Much has been written and proposed as to intensity or level of light suitable for retail stores. Brightness attracts the eye, while dimness may be passed by. Brightness, in fact, stimulates visual and emotional response and prompts action. The customer becomes a "moth," for it is known that light is an impelling and magnetic force.

But light level (degree of intensity) cannot be considered apart from the tint of illumination itself. It is one thing to be able to see clearly, and another thing to find pleasure and beauty in what is seen.

Modern studies in illumination and motivational research have emphasized the vital importance of color tint in light sources. There is unquestioned visual efficiency in mercury or sodium vapor illumination, for example, but the ugly appearance of merchandise—and human complexion—under such light sources

KALLEN'S TOWNE SHOP HAS BEIGE AND WHITE WALLS. FLOOR IS A RICH TONE-ON-TONE RED CARPET. FAR END WALL AND DECORATIVE ELEMENTS ARE GREEN. PANELS ON CABINETS ARE BRIGHT RED. THE EFFECT IS SIMPLE BUT UNIVERSALLY APPEALING. JOSE A. FERNANDEZ, ARCHITECT. PHOTOGRAPH BY ADOLPH STUDLY.

rules them out completely in store lighting. Illumination must be for appearance and not merely for acuity.

In the personal experience of the writer, undue emphasis has been given to so-called daylight. Admittedly, daylight provides the best color rendition, but it frankly isn't liked from the emotional standpoint. For, at low levels of interior illumination, the color qualities of natural daylight are likely to create a cold and forbidding atmosphere.

In practically every psychological test ever conducted to judge "pleasing" qualities in illumination, warmth has been preferred to coldness. Candlelight and firelight are far more friendly and mellow than moonlight — romance aside. Warmth in illumination flatters human complexion and gives it a ruddy glow. Cold color is cadaverous.

After all, "daylight" is an arbitrary standard in the lighting profession—equivalent to a patch of north sky in January. But natural light varies from a pinkish tint at dawn or dusk, to a warm yellow, neutral white, or delicate blue. (It is never, incidentally, greenish.)

Incandescent light is widely used in stores, both for its warm tint and for the fact that it is more directional than diffuse and hence gives form to merchandise by building up highlights and shadows. With fluorescent light, the 3500° tube is efficient, provides a lot of light and may be satisfactory under impulse buying conditions. (Daylight fluorescent is not advised.) Best of all perhaps—but not as efficient—are the so-called de luxe tubes in cool white and warm white, both of which contain red phosphors and therefore lend a warm and friendly appearance to merchandise, customers, and staff.

In summary, at low levels of illumination warm light is best and most normal. In merchandising it is ideal for products such as home furnishings because homes by and large are dimly lighted (usually with incandescent sources). Warm light at low levels also respects Kruithof's principle which has previously been discussed.

Not to overlook customer appearance, warm fluorescent or incandescent light becomes almost mandatory for personal products such as women's fashions and cosmetics. Here also the warm light should have a modeling effect in highlight and shadow and should not be too flat. Bear in mind that while cooler lighting may give colored products a realistic appearance, it may at the same time make the customer look unnatural. Sometimes it is far better to flatter the customer than the things she is buying. For if she looks bad, she may not buy anything at all!

In impulse merchandising, packaged goods, and the like really bright light—and cooler light—is well prescribed. Personal appearance may be of secondary importance. Give life and brightness to the merchandise and more of it may move off the shelves.

It would seem good policy in average retail stores to let the general illumination be warm —for the customers' benefit. Cooler sources to look more like natural daylight may then be specified over merchandise when accurate color discrimination is necessary.

IN THE JOSEPH MAGNIN, INC. STORE IN LAS VEGAS, NEVADA, THE ARCHITECTS GAVE A WESTERN FORM TO THE ARCHITECTURAL DETAILS AND MADE EXTENSIVE USE OF MOSAIC TILE AND CEMENT PLASTER. THE FREE-FLOWING PATTERNS ON WALLS ARE IN A VARIETY OF COLORS AND MARK POINTS OF INTEREST TO THE CUSTOMER TO ENCOURAGE STORE TRAFFIC. VICTOR GRUEN ASSOCIATES, ARCHITECTS. PHOTOGRAPH BY GORDON SOMMERS.

IN THE JOSEPH MAGNIN STORE IN LAS VEGAS, NEVADA, WALLS ARE SOFT TAN IN DESERT MOTIF. FLOOR IS BEIGE WITH YELLOW AND BROWN STRIPES. FREE-FORM WALL DESIGNS ARE IN GOLD AND BRIGHT RED. VICTOR GRUEN ASSOCIATES, ARCHITECTS. PHOTOGRAPH BY GORDON SOMMERS.

NOTE ON HOTELS, MOTELS, THEATERS

The decoration of hotels and motels involves many of the factors encountered in offices and stores. Therefore the colors exhibited on Charts 14 and 15 may be considered applicable. The public expects color these days—and it has good taste. As in the case of offices and stores, exceedingly high style ventures may not accomplish what management expects. Color for the sake of color holds no particular merit for, while a drab environment is emotionally discouraging, too exotic an effect may lead to rejection. The appeal of color is at unconscious levels, and people are sensitive without really knowing why. The writer has known of restaurants that have failed because of color —a deep purple in one instance. If you surround human beings with colors they innately dislike—and seldom if ever buy—you automatically sponsor distaste. A decorator can, of course, do as he wishes and be as contrary as he or his client wants, but why take the chance? After all, there are plenty of striking and compelling hues to which people respond spontaneously and favorably.

The colors of Charts 14 and 15 provide a good palette. The office colors (Chart 14), for example, lend themselves to bedrooms, parlors, sitting rooms, corridors. They could also be used for public spaces such as the lobby, although the store colors (Chart 15) are perhaps best for these areas because of their more dramatic brightness.

Suggestions for restaurants, cocktail lounges, coffee shops, cafeterias will be discussed in the next chapter and have a selection of their own on Chart 16 (page 117).

In bedrooms, parlors, suites, any number of principles may be followed. Here Oyster White (as on Chart 12) is perfectly suitable for any or all parts of a hotel or motel and is an excellent foil for brighter hues. In bedrooms, it may be applied to three walls, with the fourth wall in a deeper hue—Medium Jade, Medium Coral, Turquoise, Cocoa, Fern Green, Sapphire Blue, all on Chart 14. Or the sequence colors, instead of Oyster White, can be Sandtone, Light Warm Gray or Beige as shown on Chart 14.

For a varied, and well balanced color plan, consider the following.

CEILING IN THE LOUNGE OF CINEMA I, NEW YORK, IS BLUE. CARPET HAS SMALL BLUE AND RED SQUARES ON BLACK FIELD. FURNITURE IS UPHOLSTERED IN RED AND BLUE. ABRAHAM W. GELLER AND BEN SCHLANGER, ARCHITECTS. PHOTOGRAPH BY ALEXANDRE GEORGES.

WALLS IN CINEMA I, NEW YORK, HAVE WOOL SUEDE FABRIC COVERING. SEATS ARE A RICH RED. (THE SEATS IN CINEMA II, IN THE SAME BUILDING, ARE BLUE.) COLOR EFFECT IS SIMPLE, DRAMATIC AND OF UNIVERSAL APPEAL. ABRAHAM W. GELLER AND BEN SCHLANGER, ARCHITECTS. PHOTOGRAPH BY AEXANDRE GEORGES.

In bedrooms, use any of the light colors on Chart 14. Or combine a light neutral color with end walls in deeper tones, as just described. Or use tone-on-tone effects: Light Jade with Medium Jade. Light Coral with Medium Coral, Aqua with Turquoise, Beige with Cocoa, Sprout Green with Fern Green (as on Chart 14). Where the deeper color is used for one wall, give it generous area—such as back of beds—but never use it on window walls.

For the lobby and for public spaces, the sky is more or less the limit. However, to introduce modern trends in color, I would suggest Oyster White as a base or key note. Variety can than be added in columns, across end walls, in alcoves. Here the medium and bright hues shown in the second columns of Charts 14 and 15 are suitable. Use several colors if you wish.

In the psychological sense—and quite successful in store decoration—variety is the spice of life. Its visual and emotional action is such as to draw attention outward and have a definite (if moderate) stimulation. It invites movement and traffic.

However, if for some reason a more reserved and "cozy" atmosphere is required in a hotel or motel the overall effect can be subdued and can make use of the medium or deep colors. Be careful, however, not to repeat the vogue of the fifties in which deep greens made caverns of many a hostelry. If medium or deep colors are preferred, contrast them with light ceilings, columns, floors, furnishings, to give the eye a full sense of color values and not leave it lost in darkness. Good large area colors for a modified effect are found in Medium Jade, Medium

IN THIS BEDROOM IN THE VILLAGE GREEN MOTOR HOTEL IN COTTAGE GROVE, OREGON, THE WALLS ARE BEIGE, THE WINDOW DRAPERIES GOLD. THE BEDSPREADS ARE AQUA, WITH THE CANOPY IN SUBDUED STRIPES. CARPET IS A BEIGE TWIST. ARTHUR MORGAN. DESIGNERS.

IN THE LOUNGE OF THE VILLAGE GREEN MOTOR HOTEL IN COTTAGE GROVE, OREGON, WALLS ARE WOOD AND BRICK FOR A COMFORTABLY RUSTIC EFFECT. CARPET IS RED, UPHOLSTERY GOLD. ARTHUR MORGAN, DESIGNERS.

Coral, Turquoise, Cocoa, Fern Green and Sapphire Blue (Chart 14). Colors as deep as Forest Green, Walnut Brown, Maroon, Marine Blue, on Chart 15, are not advised over large wall areas for average hotel lighting conditions—lest trouble be encountered with Birren's principle described in Chapter XIV.

In theatres the spaces surrounding the auditorium may take specifications such as given above. The auditorium itself requires a measure of care. Here are two notes that come from personal experience.

Colors too light, such as white, may have very strong reflections. Remember that, regardless of intensity of illumination, white is always seen as white due to the phenomenon of color constancy. Stage productions or moving pictures may flood side walls near the stage

IN THE MEETING ROOM AT VILLAGE GREEN MOTOR HOTEL IN COTTAGE GROVE, OREGON, WALLS AND FLOOR ARE A SOFT WOOD IN SUBDUED STRIPES. CARPET IS A BEIGE TWIST. ARTHUR MORGAN, DESIGNERS.

HERE IS AN EXAMPLE OF A HOTEL OR MOTEL PUBLIC ROOM DESIGNED FOR A COLD CLIMATE. COLORS WITH A RUGGED AND NATURAL LOOK WOULD BE APPROPRIATE IN SUCH A ROOM AND THE WOOD, STONE, "HOMESPUN" FABRICS ARE HARMONIOUS. PHOTOGRAPH BY ALEXANDRE GEORGES.

THIS BEDROOM AT THE VILLAGE GREEN MOTOR HOTEL HAS GOLD WALLS AND UPHOLSTERED CHAIRS, LILAC BEDSPREADS, AND DEEP PURPLE CARPET. ALTHOUGH SOPHISTICATED, IT REFLECTS THE TRADITION OF THE FURNITURE. ARTHUR MORGAN, DESIGNERS.

HERE IS AN EXAMPLE OF A HOTEL OR MOTEL BEDROOM DESIGNED FOR A WARM CLIMATE. PURE AND LUMINOUS COLORS ARE BEST FOR SUNNY CLIMATES BECAUSE OF THE COMPETITION OF NATURE. WALLS AND FURNISHING ARE ON THE BRIGHT SIDE. PHOTOGRAPH BY ALEXANDRE GEORGES.

ROOM IN COLONY HOTEL IN PALM BEACH, FLORIDA, IS "WHIMSICAL VICTORIAN." WALLS AND BUREAU ARE WHITE, CARPET IS BLUE, CHAIR AQUA. BEDSPREADS ARE PURPLE AND WHITE. PIERO ARERSA, DESIGNER. PHOTOGRAPH COURTESY MARTIAL INTERNATIONAL.

IN THE ISLANDIA MOTEL AT MISSION BAY, SAN DIEGO, CALIFORNIA, BRIGHT, TROPICAL PASTELS ARE BROUGHT INSIDE FOR A CHEERFUL, "HOLIDAY," EFFECT. EUGENE WESTON, JR., FREDERICK LIEBHARDT, EUGENE WESTON, III, ARCHITECTS. LA JOLLA INTERIORS, WILLIS SHORT, INTERIOR DESIGNERS, PHOTOGRAPH BY JULIUS SHULMAN.

or screen with unfavorable and disturbing brightness if white is employed here.

Colors too deep, on the other hand, may get completely "lost" in dim illumination for reasons of color constancy given in Chapter XIV. While a fair appearance may exist with lights on, when lights are down the dark-colored walls may fade out into a "nothingness" and give the interior a weird atmosphere.

Good colors for theatre interiors, therefore, are in the medium range. Suggested are Medium Coral, Turquoise, Cocoa, and Fern Green (Chart 14). Not to be too severe, some trim or details—such as the overhead and the undersides of balconies—may be in lighter tones of the same hues. Or the trim and overhead may be neutral Sandtone or Light Warm Gray (Chart 14). Medium Coral and Cocoa will provide a "warm" feeling and a cheerful and friendly one, while Turquoise and Fern Green will be psychologically cool.

If different colors are wanted on different walls, the two sides of the auditorium should be the same, while a different color (or two different colors) may be applied to the area surrounding the stage or screen and to the back of the theater.

MOST FURNITURE, TEXTILES, RUGS IN THIS BEDROOM IN THE HOTEL MONT-PARNES, GREECE, ARE OF NATIVE DESIGN. WALL COLORS ARE PLAIN AND OFFSET BY RESTRAINED TOUCHES OF BRIGHT COLOR IN FURNISHINGS AND ACCESSORIES. PAUL M. NYLONAS, ARCHITECT.

AUDITORIUM OF HARBORFIELDS CENTRAL HIGH SCHOOL, GREEN-LAWN, NEW YORK HAS A WHITE CEILING, BEIGE FLOOR, SOFT GRAY WALLS, BLUE STAGE CURTAIN. AN UNUSUAL FEATURE IS FOUND IN DIFFERENT SHADES OF BLUE FOR SEATS. THIS FACILITATES EASY REPAIR WITHOUT NEED FOR EXACT MATCHING. J. STANLEY SHARP, PARTNER IN CHARGE, KETCHUM & SHARP, ARCHITECTS. PHOTOGRAPH BY G. AMIAGA.

Color as related to food and food service poses a number of interesting psychological problems. Eating is one of America's leading pastimes. Color is forever a part of food, a visual element to which human eyes, minds, emotions, and palates are mighty sensitive.

First the food itself, the lush reds, mellow browns, the greens and yellows and orange tints of vegetables and fruits. Then the package or container in which it is featured, the store or market in which it is displayed, the restaurant or home in which it is served, the napery, china—even the carpets, walls, furniture which provide the setting.

There is a definite art of color in food which is important to those who merchandise it and to those who willingly or reluctantly consume it. What may not be too well appreciated is the fact that a sizable amount of research has been devoted to the matter of color and food, and much of it has direct and practical application.

It may seem a bit farfetched to speak of physiological responses to color as they relate to appetite. But it really is not. One maker of chocolate candy found that sugar coating in a variety of hues (all with the same flavor) sold better than plain white or brown. Few consumers know that butter—the expensive spread—is tinted for color control, just as is oleomargarine. Butter that is too white may resemble lard, and butter that is too "goldenrod" may appear rancid. People demand the right shade (in countless other foodstuffs as well) and will accept or reject a product on its appearance—nutrition aside.

Perhaps basic to color and appetite are certain direct associations and certain known re-

VIEW SHOWS RESTAURANT AT ST. FRANCIS HOTEL, SEATTLE. ARTHUR MORGAN, DESIGNERS.

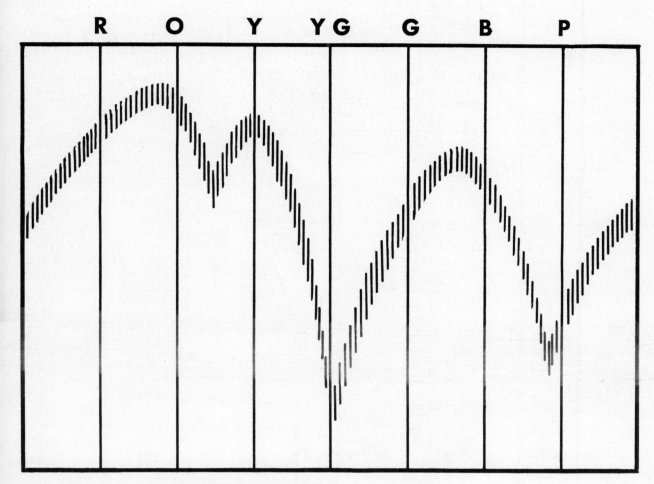

THIS CHART SHOWS THE APPEAL OF COLOR TO THE APPETITE.
NOTE THE PEAKS THAT OCCUR IN RED, ORANGE, YELLOW, AND
GREEN, WITH LOW POINTS IN YELLOW-GREEN AND PURPLE. BLUE,
WHILE NOT DIRECTLY ASSOCIATED WITH FOODS, IS NONE THE
LESS A GOOD FOIL FOR THEM.

sponses to the stimulation of color. Bright and warm colors (red, orange, yellow) tend to stimulate what is known as the autonomic nervous system of man, including digestion, while soft and cool colors tend to retard it. In experiments with birds and animals it has been found that reddish or yellowish light will excite hunger, while blue and green light will discourage it.

In psychological studies of appetite appeal in color, a specific food "palette" is clearly revealed. While not all persons will "feel" the same about colors or have the same reactions, by and large there are common denominators worthy of attention from the food industry.

Refer to the accompanying chart which plots average responses of pleasure and displeasure in color as associated with foods.

A peak is reached in the red-orange and orange region of the spectrum where such hues seem to arouse the most agreeable sensations. There is a drop off at yellow-orange and a pickup at yellow. Toward yellow-green, however, a low point is found. While yellow-green may seem fashionable enough as applied to clothing or home furnishings, it is "distasteful" as applied to foods.

Pleasure is again restored in cool green and blue-green, followed by another drop when purples are considered.

Most readers will perhaps agree with these conclusions, psychological though they are. There is good appetite in red, red-orange, peach, pink, tan, brown, "butter" yellow, light and clear green. Blue-greens, while seldom associated with food itself, none the less are well

THE BEEF 'N BIRD TAVERN IN THE HOTEL KENMORE, BOSTON, HAS BEEN DESIGNED BY HOTEL CORPORATION OF AMERICA UNDER THE DIRECTION OF ROLAND W. JUTRAS. VIEW SHOWS PART OF BAR AND LOUNGE. WALLS ARE OF OLD BRICK AND BARNWOOD. CEILING IS STAINED BROWN. UPHOLSTERY IS IN RED LEATHER. PHOTOGRAPH BY LOUIS REENS.

regarded and well liked—and suggest an ideal foil or background to the display of food. Colors such as the above will be found shown on Chart 16.

Poor colors are found in purplish reds, purple, violet, yellow-green, greenish yellow, orange yellow, gray and most olive and "mustardy" tones.

There are other fine points which sensitive mortals will express. Pink seems sweet. Candy colors suggest pastels. Wines are liked in pink, golden yellow, claret red.

The same appetite colors do not apply to all foods. Colored bread, once introduced, failed completely. While "pretty" colors seem appropriate to cake frostings and cookies, they would be heartily rejected if used for mashed potatoes. A glass of purple grape juice would be relished—but a purple gravy or consomme would certainly not be.

Colors for foods involve personal and emotional interpretations. No generalizations can be accepted as absolute. Nevertheless, it is good "business" to avoid personal views for a more objective approach to the way in which *most* persons seem to react.

Now for some recommended specifications. Refer to the color standards on Chart 16.

In food stores, good wall colors for the interior at large would be Peach or Light Spring Green—with Melon or Medium Spring Green for lower areas or feature purposes. Good accents for display would be Warm Yellow, Vermilion, Melon, Flamingo, Cascade Blue.

Light and Medium Aquamarine are suggested for areas in and around meats, with the meats themselves placed perhaps on white trays. Aquamarine will, by direct visual complementation, give meats a pinker and more appetizing look. In some stores, pink light has been used over meats and soft green light over vegetables to emphasize natural colors.

Food display racks are probably best in White, Light or Medium Aquamarine. If practical, the backs of racks and shelving should be white to reflect abundant light and to set up a

THE CHRISTIANA AT KETCHUM, IDAHO, HAS THIS INTIMATE COCK-
TAIL LOUNGE AND RESTAURANT. TERRY & MOORE, ARCHITECTS.
PHOTOGRAPH BY DEARBORN-MASSAR.

DUBLIN HOUSE, SEATTLE, DESIGNED BY TERRY & MOORE, ARCHITECTS, HAS A GENERALLY DEEP ENVIRONMENT, WITH CANDLELIGHT ON INDIVIDUAL TABLES. THIS TENDS TO CONCENTRATE ATTENTION ON ROOM DETAILS—AND CUSTOMERS. PHOTOGRAPH BY DEARBORN-MASSAR.

HERE IS ANOTHER VIEW OF THE WELL-DESIGNED RESTAURANT AT DUBLIN HOUSE, SEATTLE. NOTE HOW ATTENTION GOES TO TABLES AND WALL DECORATION. ILLUMINATION IS SOFT AND WARM. TERRY & MOORE, ARCHITECTS. PHOTOGRAPH BY DEARBORN-MASSAR.

strong contrast with packaged goods.

For restaurants, cafeterias, coffee shops, lunch counters, a number of principles are to be considered. For a lunch counter, coffee shop, or cafeteria, for example, a bright and stimulating environment will draw trade, invite action, pep up appetites, and help to keep business humming. Here warm and luminous wall colors are proposed, such as Peach, Melon, Warm Yellow. The wall back of a counter or serving area could be Melon, Vermilion, or Flamingo to delight the eye. The counters themselves and the fronts of the serving tables could be a contrasting Medium Aquamarine or Cascade Blue.

In restaurants with table service a more refined atmosphere may be wanted. Here ideal wall colors would be Light or Medium Spring Green, Beach Tan, Coffee Brown. Always be careful of white or off-white on walls. The effect is not only "sterile," but it may cause a glare condition that will, through brightness-

THE LONDON CLUB AT TWA TERMINAL, IDLEWILD AIRPORT, NEW YORK, AN UNUSUAL BUILDING BY ONE OF AMERICA'S GREAT MODERN ARCHITECTS (EERO SAARINEN). LOEWY/SNAITH, INC., DESIGNERS. PHOTOGRAPH BY GOTTSCHO-SCHLEISNER.

THIS IS THE LISBON LOUNGE AT TWA TERMINAL, IDLEWILD AIRPORT, NEW YORK. LOEWY/SNAITH, INC., DESIGNERS. PHOTOGRAPH BY GOTTSCHO-SCHLEISNER.

contrast, give foods (and the people eating them) a dull appearance.

In a cocktail lounge or dining room where illumination is usually on the dim side, wall colors can be fairly rich—such as Medium Spring Green, Coffee Brown, Medium Aquamarine, Cascade Blue. Vermilion and Flamingo are also excellent if there are table lamps and if walls are not brightly illuminated.

In fact, if the colors of Chart 16 are kept in view, a sprightly and appetizing environment will be assured.

Finally, there is the matter of illumination. High levels in stores have been profitable in impulse buying when the emphasis is on the foods displayed and not on the customer. Here attention is directed outward to that which is being sold. If anything, such brilliant light should be either neutral white or slightly on the warm side—never bluish.

In food service, however, warm light is next

to imperative. The most savory meal would be rejected if served under mercury or sodium vapor light. (This has been tested and proved.) A new principle in restaurants is to have a versatile lighting installation in which a bright flood can be used for the noon hour rush, and a soft diffusion of warmth for the evening dinner. In one instance the brilliance of the environment pulls the hungry mortal into the establishment and out in a hurry, while in the other the homelike or intimate atmosphere invites relaxation and repose—and a big check.

IN A MORE FORMAL DINING ROOM AT THE VILLAGE GREEN MOTOR HOTEL IN OREGON, WOOD, BRICK AND COPPER ON SURROUNDING WALLS AND FIREPLACE HOOD GIVE A WARM AND MELLOW ATMOSPHERE. THE CARPET AND UPHOLSTERY ARE A WARM RED. ARTHUR MORGAN, DESIGNERS.

IN THE COFFEE SHOP OF THE VILLAGE GREEN MOTOR HOTEL, OREGON, A WARM, APPETIZING EFFECT IS ACHIEVED THROUGH THE USE OF RED ON WALLS AND UPHOLSTERY, WITH TRIM IN IVORY. THE ORNATE LIGHTING FIXTURES LEND A VICTORIAN TOUCH. ARTHUR MORGAN, DESIGNERS.

THIS BAR AND RESTAURANT IN EL CONVENTO HOTEL IN SAN JUAN, PUERTO RICO, HAS BEEN DECORATED ON THE BRIGHT SIDE FOR APPEAL TO AVERAGE TOURISTS. PHOTOGRAPH BY ALEXANDRE GEORGES.

21 PERSONAL PREFERENCE IN HOMES

Assuming that a home is a man's—and a woman's—castle where freedom reigns, any of the colors presented in this book could be chosen. If there is a sympathy for the traditional, there are precedents to be observed. If modernity is wanted, the color charts in the latter part of the book (12 to 16) are open for reference.

The decoration of homes is and should be a personal affair. Despite many years of experience in the *functional* specifications of color for commercial and institutional interiors, the author is ever reluctant to offer advice regarding a home. It is often much easier to do five or six floors of general business space than to settle the details of a private office. People will listen to reason when devoting attention to the needs of others, but they will take exception to personal intrusions on their own conceptions of taste.

This is as it should be—but not always is. Most human beings have deep feelings about color. Their attitude toward it may be like their religions or political convictions—not to be disturbed without a strong emotional response. No color scheme to my knowledge, no interior, holds universal appeal. Tradition may seem archaic to a modern, and modernism may seem ludicrous to a fancier of period styles. As to color itself, differences of view are even more pronounced. Almost every hue has its "lovers" and "haters." And when one person uses what another person dislikes, this second mortal may secretly or openly wonder at the wretched taste of the first.

There could be a "scientific" way of decorating a home, but very few would like it. For

THE COLOR SCHEME OF THIS LIVING ROOM IS CHIEFLY IN TONES OF BEIGE (CARPET, DRAPERIES) ACCENTED BY RED, ORANGE, AND GOLD IN UPHOLSTERY. THE LEATHER CHAIR IS BLACK. PHOTOGRAPH COURTESY JANE J. GRAHAM.

THIS INTERIOR, ON THE BRIGHT SIDE, HAS OFF-WHITE ON WALLS AND IN DRAPERIES AND UPHOLSTERY. THERE IS DRAMATIC ACCENT IN THE ABSTRACT PAINTING AND CARPET. PHOTOGRAPH COURTESY WINDOW SHADE MANUFACTURERS ASSOCIATION.

IN THIS INFORMAL ROOM THERE IS GOOD USE OF NATURAL MATERIALS—GOLD PANELLED WALLS, SMOKED TEAK BEAMS, NATURAL STONE FIREPLACE. THE FLOOR IS BRONZE GREEN. BRIGHT ACCENTS ARE IN DRAPERIES, RUG, CUSHIONS. AMOREAL KAMINS, DESIGNER. PHOTOGRAPH BY VERN AND ELIZABETH GREEN.

WALLS IN THIS HOUSE IN BEVERLY HILLS, CALIFORNIA, ARE PALE MAUVE, CARPET WHITE, SHUTTERS GOLDEN YELLOW. THE MARBLE IS WHITE WITH GRAY VEINING. ORIGINAL DESIGN BY PAUL LASZLO. PHOTOGRAPH BY JULIUS SHULMAN.

THIS IS A BREAKFAST AREA IN A HOUSE IN BEVERLY HILLS, CALIFORNIA. WALLS AND FLOOR ARE OFF-WHITE, SHUTTERS ALTERNATE RED AND WHITE. CHAIRS ARE WHITE WITH BRILLIANT RED UPHOLSTERY. ORIGINAL DESIGN BY PAUL LASZLO. PHOTOGRAPH BY ROBERT C. CLEVELAND.

example, the living room could, with good cause, be a medium tone of rose to create a soft, warm, and cheerful atmosphere. The dining room could be in some of the colors of Chart 16, perhaps with peach walls and turquoise blue furnishings to inspire appetites. The kitchen could be in yellow with red and blue accents to establish a lively effect and make time pass swiftly. The bedroom could be in pink or aqua like spring itself. But who would care? Logic does not usually prevail where color and human personality are involved. The "soul" must be satisfied, and, as is well known, no two souls are alike.

It seems important for a person to get his own way with color. Advice can be accepted on matters of design, form, arrangement—or even help on the particular tone of a color for a particular setting. But *the color itself* ought to come from the heart. If it does not, the home owner may well end up dissatisfied if not distraught and unhappy.

IN THIS BEDROOM IN A HOUSE IN SEATTLE, WASHINGTON, END WALL IS BLUISH VIOLET. CARPET IS OFF-WHITE, BEDSPREADS A DELICATE PINK. UPHOLSTERY IS A COMPLEMENTARY RED. ARTHUR MORGAN, DESIGNERS.

Some years ago, the author conceived the word *psychodecor*. He has written one book and numerous articles on the psychological and psychiatric aspects of color. In the process he has learned much about the subtle peculiarities of the human psyche.

For example, and in a broad sense, people may be classified as extroverts and introverts. The terms are those of Carl Jung. The extroverts by nature are outgoing and take delight in bright and warm colors. The introverts, on the other hand, are more introspective and likely to prefer subdued and cool colors. In a similar way, it is natural for extroverts to like innovation and modernism in furniture, while the introvert, needing reason to support his taste, may prefer the sentiment and historic dignity attached to that which is traditional. Certainly, no one is "right" or "wrong" here, for no amount of debate could settle anything.

One hazards much to give advice on color. A timid person might be told to use bright colors and get over his moody ways. Yet bright colors can make this person so extremely self-conscious that he may become even more timid and lugubrious. The excitable person, advised to surround himself with soft and subdued hues, may find that such an environment "bottles up" his spirit and makes him all the more nervous. Incidentally, these facts are known in the field of psychiatry, and principles based on them are used in the decoration of elementary schools, general and mental hospitals.

So it is poor wisdom to let the individuality of others impose on your own. There is deep and profound satisfaction in color that is well worth the emotional effort of bringing it forth. Architects and interior decorators should consider it part of their trade to "psychoanalyze" their clients. (The good ones do.) Color can make people happy—and unhappy. Where attention is given to human predilections, to a skillful and talented interpretation of the heart-felt desires of others, decoration be-

comes a high art. It is inspired to great original-ity and variety, for it takes on shades of expression as diverse as those that go to make up human character.

If advice is to be given, let it get down to the facts, phenomena, and case-history experi-ences which affect the use of any and all colors. Here are a few notes and observations.

Colors will turn out a good bit more intense in large area than in small. The color of a paint chip or on a color card will not appear the same on a wall. (In the samples on the charts of this book, however, allowance has been made for this; some that may look dull are purposely so for their end use.)

Be particularly careful of pale luminous colors like yellow. They are most deceptive in a chip. On the walls of a room, and because of high reflectance, the light colors will "bounce" back and forth and hence increase in purity. For example, if a cheerful yellow (or lime, peach, or pink) is wanted, choose the chip and then dilute the paint with as much as fifty per cent white—the color on the chip and that on the wall will then probably look the same.

THIS IS THE SUMMER SCHEME OF WORK BEDROOM AT DRAGON ROCK, HOME OF EMINENT DESIGNER, RUSSEL WRIGHT. WALL AT RIGHT IS WHITE URETHANE FOAM. CEILING IS DEEP GREEN WITH WEATHERED BEAMS. ACCENTS ARE BRIGHT IN FLOOR MAT, BED-SPREAD, PILLOWS. RUSSEL WRIGHT, DESIGNER. PHOTOGRAPH BY ALEXANDRE GEORGES.

THIS INTERESTING NOOK COMBINES A VARIETY OF OLD AND NEW OBJECTS. WALLS ARE A DEEP, TRADITIONAL GOLD WITH WHITE TRIM. PERSONALITY IS EXPRESSED HERE IN A HARMONY OF THINGS FROM WIDELY DIFFERENT SOURCES. PHOTOGRAPH BY ALEXANDRE GEORGES.

Don't fear pure colors, such as red. While they may not stand full daylight, in a normal interior with draperies, blinds, and artificial light, they will soften down. If you really like color, do not deprive yourself. If four walls are too many, put the brilliant color on one and a neutral on the others.

If deep colors are preferred, use similar precautions and keep in mind Birren's principle described in Chapter XIV. In an artificially lit room the dark color can stand some reflected light. During the day it will be perfectly all right. However, be cautious about dark colors (or brilliant ones) on ceilings. They may crowd down in a disturbing way.

Above all, and in a home, have the courage of your convictions and feelings. Color is one of the natural delights of this world. It is the rule of nature, not the exception, and there is much of the good life in it.

THE END

THIS INFORMAL DINING NOOK, MOSTLY IN NATURAL MATERIALS,
HAS A UNIQUE VERTICAL RIBBON ROOM DIVIDER ON A TRACK.
WOODS CAN BE BEAUTIFULLY HARMONIZED WITH TONES OF GOLD,
FERN GREEN, ORANGE. PHOTOGRAPH BY ALEXANDRE GEORGES.

ACKNOWLEDGMENTS

Thanks are expressed for the considerable help extended to the author in the preparation of this book. Chapter XIII, on quantity and quality of illumination, represents so much work on the part of H. L. Logan as to be, actually, a collaborative effort with the author. To Mrs. William Hale Kirby for extensive historical research and assistance in the collection of pictures. To Mrs. Elschen Hood for a survey of color and textiles on Renaissance, French and English traditions. To the New York Public Library, The Metropolitan Museum, The Art Institute of Chicago, The Winterthur Museum, and other sources for their good cooperation.

Numerous books and publications have also been consulted. However, there are very few works devoted exclusively to color in historic decoration. The following three are notable:

The British Colour Council Dictionary of Colours for Interior Decoration, London, 1949.

Historical Colours, Thos. Parsons & Sons Ltd., London, 1934.

Elizabeth Burris-Meyer, Historical Color Guide, William Helburn, Inc., New York, 1938.

INDEX

This book is designed by Patrick Norado
assisted by John R. Czerkowicz.
It is set in Linotype Palatino supplied
by Haber Typographers.
Printing is by Robert Teller Sons & Dorner.
Binding is by the Russell-Rutter Company.
The paper used for the text is Optone Gardenia,
designed by Faber Birren for the Whiteford Paper Co.
and made by the Rising Paper Co. Optone papers
are covered by U. S. Patent 2,916,304.